*Designing and Developing*
# Programs for
# Gifted Students

To all those pioneering individuals—known and unknown—who
have devoted themselves to creating programs that transform the lives
of gifted children and young people. Also to my own staff and teachers at
the Center for Gifted at National-Louis University for their untiring
commitment to the thousands of gifted students in the Chicago
area who come for challenge and inspiration.

# Designing and Developing
# Programs for
# Gifted Students

# Joan Franklin Smutny, EDITOR

A Service Publication of the National Association for Gifted Children

**CORWIN PRESS, INC.**
A Sage Publications Company
Thousand Oaks, California

KH

*For information:*

 Corwin Press, Inc.
A Sage Publications Company
2455 Teller Road
Thousand Oaks, California 91320
www.corwinpress.com

Sage Publications Ltd.
6 Bonhill Street
London EC2A 4PU
United Kingdom

Sage Publications India Pvt. Ltd.
M-32 Market
Greater Kailash I
New Delhi 110 048 India

Printed in the United States of America

**Library of Congress Cataloging-in-Publication Data**

Designing and developing programs for gifted students / by Joan Franklin Smutny, editor.
  p. cm.
Published in cooperation with the National Association for Gifted Children, Inc.
Includes bibliographical references and index.
ISBN 0-7619-3852-4 — ISBN 0-7619-3853-2 (pbk.)
  1. Gifted children-Education (Elementary)—United States. 2. Gifted children-Education (Middle school)—United States. 3. Curriculum planning-United States. I. Smutny, Joan F. II. Title.
LC3993.22 .D47 2003
371.95´0973—dc21

2002013045

This book is printed on acid-free paper.

03  04  05  06   10  9  8  7  6  5  4  3  2

| | |
|---|---|
| *Acquisitions Editor:* | Robert D. Clouse |
| *Editorial Assistant:* | Erin Clow |
| *Production Editor:* | Diana E. Axelsen |
| *Cover Designer:* | Tracy Miller |
| *Production Artist:* | Michelle Lee |
| *Indexer:* | Judy Hunt |

10/25/04

# *Contents*

# *Acknowledgments*

Corwin Press gratefully acknowledges the contributions of the following reviewer: James J. Gallagher, W. R. Kenan Jr. Distinguished Professor, School of Education, University of North Carolina at Chapel Hill.

# *About the Editor*

**Joan Franklin Smutny** is the founder and Director of the Center for Gifted at National-Louis University and also teaches gifted education courses to graduate students. The Center for Gifted offers programs to thousands of gifted children from all socioeconomic and cultural backgrounds—age 4 through Grade 10. In 1996, she won the National Association for Gifted Children (NAGC) Distinguished Service Award for outstanding contributions to the field of gifted education. She has authored, coauthored, and edited nine books on gifted education, including *Teaching Young Gifted Children in the Regular Classroom* (1997), *The Young Gifted Child: An Anthology* (1998), *Gifted Girls* (1998), *Stand Up for Your Gifted Child* (2001), and *Underserved Gifted Populations* (2002). She has written many articles and is a contributing editor for *Understanding Our Gifted* and *Roeper Review*.

# About the Contributors

**Cheryll M. Adams** is the Director of the Center for Gifted Studies and Talent Development at Ball State University and teaches classes in gifted education. She was formerly a science and math teacher for 15 years in both public and private schools. Formerly affiliated with the National Research Center on the Gifted and Talented at the University of Virginia, she has published and presented widely in the field, is coeditor of NAGC *Research Briefs,* and is a former member of the Board of Directors of NAGC. She is the first vice president of the Indiana Association for the Gifted and editor of *IMAGES,* the IAG journal.

**Deborah E. Bordelon** is Assistant Professor of Education at Xavier University of Louisiana and teaches courses in the area of gifted and talented. Her commitment to gifted education extends beyond the university level. She has taught extensively in gifted programs at the elementary and middle school levels and currently coordinates a summer program for academically gifted students.

**Ruth Erken** has acquired extensive knowledge and expertise in education from Bonn, Cologne, and Nijmegen (the Netherlands). She has designed and developed enrichment programs for gifted children in Germany as well as counseling services for parents. In 2001, she was chairperson of a conference with representatives from the different German school ministries to coordinate schoolwide gifted education programs (Germany is a federal republic with 16 school ministries). She has also published on the special needs of gifted girls.

**Christopher M. Freeman** teaches at the University of Chicago Laboratory Schools, where he especially enjoys providing enrichment activities for mathematically gifted 6th graders. He has 16 years of experience teaching mathematics to students in Grades 6 through 12. He spends his summers and winter weekends teaching gifted children ages 8 through 15 in the

Worlds of Wisdom and Wonder and Project gifted programs administered by the Center for Gifted at National-Louis University. He is also the author of a book of math games, *Nim: Variations and Strategies* (2001).

**Patricia L. Hollingsworth** is Director of the University School at the University of Tulsa, where she also teaches art and kindergarten. She has been with the school since 1982. She has also served as a member of the NAGC Board of Directors for a number of years, is on the Advisory Board of *Understanding Our Gifted*, and is a contributing editor of the *Roeper Review*. She is the coauthor of *Smart Art* and *Kinetic Kaleidoscope*, two books on art for children. She was the editor and a contributing author of the *SAILS* books.

**Eileen Kelble** has expertise in the fields of counseling and gifted education. For a number of years, she served on the faculty at the University of Tulsa, where she also worked on grants in gifted education and science and acted as a principal investigator for many workshops, summer academies, and other programs for teachers and students. She started the Master's Program in Gifted at the university and was instrumental in the founding of several private schools. She has served as cochair of the Special Schools and Programs Division of NAGC and has retired from full-time teaching. Her most recent publication focuses on schools for gifted, published by NAGC and Corwin Press.

**Cheryl Lind** is Associate Director of the Center for Gifted at National-Louis University. A trained child psychologist, she also tests and evaluates gifted children and guides parents on appropriate courses of action for meeting their unique educational needs. In addition to her administrative responsibilities and expertise in testing gifted students, she has also taught in a number of Center for Gifted programs.

**Norman J. Mirman** is the founder and Director Emeritus of the Mirman School for Gifted Children in Los Angeles. His advanced education and expertise at UCLA led him to devote his life to teaching gifted children at the elementary and middle school levels and to the founding of his school. He has also lectured on gifted education to parent groups and at various universities throughout the Southern California area. His most recent article, titled "A Modern Day Guide for the Perplexed," appeared in the spring issue of the *Gifted Child Communicator*. His pioneering contribution to gifted education is well known throughout the field.

**Sara Delano Moore** is Director of the Kentucky Center for Middle School Academic Achievement, based at Eastern Kentucky University. With expertise in the field of gifted education at the University of Virginia, she has taught in both public and independent schools, primarily in middle school science. She has also worked in mathematics programs for gifted students through the Center for Talented Youth at Johns Hopkins University as a teacher, mathematics coordinator, and academic dean.

**Pam Piskurich** is the Program Coordinator for Carnegie Mellon University's C-MITES (Carnegie Mellon Institute for Talented Elementary Students) program. She plans and organizes workshops and programs for both students and parents as well as special training for teachers interested in gifted education. She assists with the publication of the *C-MITES News* for students, educators, and parents. She taught math at the middle and high school level over a 14-year period and also wrote an eighth-grade math curriculum and many interdisciplinary thematic team units. She has presented at the Pennsylvania Association for Gifted Education, the National Association for Gifted Children, and the National Council for Teachers of Mathematics conferences. She coauthored an article published in *The Gifted Child Today* magazine.

**Mary K. Pleiss** has expertise in both elementary education and gifted education. She is the former Director of Purdue's Super Saturday program for gifted students. Now a fourth-grade teacher at the Sycamore School for the gifted in Indianapolis, Indiana, she continues to publish articles, present at conferences, develop curricula, and write original fiction. Her students teach her daily that flexibility and a sense of humor are essential when putting research into practice.

**Maria Lucia Sabatella** is a professional educator, consultant, and researcher who specializes in gifted education. Her graduate work was in education from the Federal University of Parana-Curitiba, Brazil. She founded the Institute for Learning Optimization as a pioneer initiative, with the purpose of designing a pattern of identification procedures for giftedness that best suits the educational opportunities in her country. Today, the institute is working with parent groups, preparing teachers, and providing educational alternatives that will serve the gifted students' special needs.

**CORWIN PRESS**

The Corwin Press logo—a raven striding across an open book—represents the happy union of courage and learning. We are a professional-level publisher of books and journals for K-12 educators, and we are committed to creating and providing resources that embody these qualities. Corwin's motto is "Success for All Learners."

# Introduction

*Joan Franklin Smutny*

Gifted programs have the potential to change lives. This may seem an exaggeration to some, but we, the authors, have seen it. We have watched bored and apathetic students reenergized by learning a new subject, exploring a fresh theory or angle, or testing a hypothesis they discovered in a gifted program. We have seen artistic and imaginative children, neglected in the regular classroom, come to life in a place where they can use their creative strengths in art, creative writing, theater, and dance. When developed with care and nurtured at each step, gifted programs bring hope and the promise of new possibility to talented children who need this kind of intervention.

The many attempts of researchers and of society to define the word *gifted* are too numerous and varied to explore in any detail in this Introduction. However, this seemingly innocuous definition is the most important philosophical underpinning of any gifted program. Perhaps the best identifier of the gifted individual relates not so much to what degree or type of gift he or she has *received* but to what degree or type of gift this child passionately desires *to give*. Gifted children are almost uniformly zealous in their aspirations to share knowledge and understanding gained with others and with the world. This may find manifestation in the child who can't stop talking to everyone about dinosaurs, the child who cries over reports of unrest in the evening news broadcast, or the seeming perfectionism of the child who has invested himself or herself heavily in his or her work. Emerson's (1844) quip, "The only gift is a portion of thyself," rings true among these children and young people.

Gifted programs allow gifted children to share their insights and talents—*to be gifted*—in ways their usual classrooms rarely can. The result of this is lasting satisfaction and improved self-esteem on the part of the children, accompanied by an even greater thirst for future achievement. It is this facet of *giving* that explains why so many gifted children find themselves transformed by programs.

1

Much has been written on gifted classes. This book, however, focuses on gifted *programs*. The distinction is important. A *gifted program* might be defined as the following:

> A class or set of classes spanning a time frame less than a school year, offered to children as an option beyond what is available in the regular classroom and in which students of similar talent are grouped together to the exclusion of other students, in order to allow (a) the optimization of educational outcomes through communicative spillovers or synergies across students and between teachers and students, (b) the teaching of more in-depth or accelerated material to students *as a group*, and (c) the provision of an environment where scholarship and other educational outcomes such as socialization are complements, not substitutes.

A program for gifted children must be exclusionary—namely, it must emphasize grouping of like-talented students. The exclusion may be done using a variety of different criteria, including by self-selection, but it must be done at some level. This is because it is grouping that essentially provides the raison d'être for gifted programs of all sorts. Both theory and evidence document that high-ability students receive greater benefits, or "spillovers," from having high-ability peers than do low-ability students. Under this condition, the talent sorting that programs for the gifted provide offers an improvement on the aggregate outcomes of an educational system. "Spillovers" in talent are well documented and psychologically based, and the chapter in this volume by Maria Sabatella discusses the psychological literature in greater detail. Moreover, in the most recent study on the subject, Hoxby (2000) used a very large panel of data on Texas elementary school students to provide further evidence on the size of talent spillovers, suggesting that a 1% improvement in peer talent levels generates between .1% and .4% improvements in any individual student's educational outcomes. Most of the empirical research on this subject has necessarily focused on test scores as educational outcomes, but it is not difficult to imagine that equally large or larger spillovers exist for the far broader outcomes that genuinely determine student achievement, success, and satisfaction in education. Those interested in a more detailed survey of theoretical and empirical work on grouping may wish to consult Kulik and Kulik (1991).

Both gifted programs and gifted classes within school settings are predicated on the benefits of grouping. In addition to these effects, however, programs also feature some other benefits not generally available in classes. Programs offer the opportunity for in-depth, rigorous, and intensive study of particular subjects of interest to gifted children in ways that even gifted classes within school settings often cannot. According to *The Gifted Kid's Survival Guide*, the number one "great gripe" of gifted kids is that "the stuff we do in school is too easy and it's boring" (Galbraith, 1983). Gifted children love to take hold of an idea and wring it dry like a wet towel, extracting every possible insight it offers. Where the regular classroom offers a limited investigation of issues unimportant to children, gifted programs allow students to vigorously seek fundamental truths about the questions they ask, overcoming the doubt or mistrust in themselves as scholars and thinkers that LeVine and Kitano (1998) identified as a primary stumbling block for gifted children. Many researchers have identified the opportunity to pursue their own fervent learning interests as the most useful educational strategy of gifted individuals (e.g., Clark, 1992; Cohen, 1998). Moreover, the regular mixed-talent classroom must often focus solely on method, drill, and repetition, whereas the motivation, interest, and high ability of gifted students allow for a program that focuses on application, offering opportunities for higher-level thinking, transdisciplinary study (Drake, 1998), and real-world "Type III" investigations (Renzulli & Reis, 1986). Thus, gifted programs offer students a break from an often dreary experience in school, freeing them from the lockhold imposed by a classroom setting based on state and district standards that all students must meet. Gifted children are then allowed to share their talents more deeply, and they often take away from the experience new insights into how they can continue to give of themselves on a larger level after the end of the program.

Gifted programs also provide students with an opportunity to network with children who are similarly talented but raised in different environments. The primary critique of grouping, and hence of gifted education, is that it may involve an "ivory tower" effect, wherein children who have been grouped together all their lives never learn to communicate with others outside the group. Galbraith (1983) stated it more bluntly: "Myth #6: If GTs [gifted and talented] are grouped together, they'll become snobs or elitist" (p. 21). Gifted programs bring students out of their regularly scheduled classrooms—whether gifted, differentiated, or undifferentiated—and place them in new settings, with new teachers, new subjects, and, typically, new peers. The result is higher achievement, not only in academic pursuits but also in interpersonal communication and relations. Because gifted children desire above all to share their talents, the development of communication skills is highly important to their long-term development and potential.

For a particular program to achieve these deep and broad benefits to students and to society, we must remember the practical considerations of development and implementation. Although the authors represented in this book all bring different areas of expertise to this subject, we are united in our recognition of the following:

1. Gifted programs should not simply offer enrichment but a cohesive, rigorous, creative, and in-depth course of study.

2. Gifted programs should use the best possible teachers in the subjects offered.

3. Gifted programs should accommodate children with different learning styles, cultures, and socioeconomic backgrounds.

4. Gifted programs should counsel children and families who need help with emotional, social, and other problems commonly associated with giftedness.

Many different learning experiences fall under the definition of a "gifted program." This book offers examples of several. Summer camp for highly gifted mathematics students, weekend poetry courses, afterschool theater settings, and an infinite variety of other offerings might all be classified as gifted programs. This book makes no attempt to be exhaustive; it does not need to be. We could have presented a detailed blueprint or a set of formulas that everyone should follow, yet this would ignore all the differences that exist between programs and the communities they serve—differences in philosophy, in resources, and in populations. Our aim instead has been to present the basic elements and operating principles that make gifted programs effective, creative, and continuous. It is our hope that you, the readers, will find in this volume the inspiration and practical guidance you need to start your own gifted programs or at least to apply the ideas here to programs you already have. Beyond this, it is up to you to assess what works best in your experience and how you should approach each phase of program development based on the resources available and the people involved.

Given the relatively low priority placed on gifted education and the inadequate services most of these children receive in the United States and abroad, gifted programs help fill a void for the nation's gifted students. To help them become strong leaders for the future, program developers of all kinds need to grapple with the larger question: How can we do more for gifted children? This book provides many answers, but perhaps the most important is that the people involved in different kinds of gifted programs should do more to work together. This would mean not merely supporting each other's efforts but creating partnerships that would benefit the children who need more than an occasionally stimulating class. By themselves, programs offer only a part-time solution, but giftedness is a full-time condition. Together, however, they could create a more comprehensive and systematic approach to gifted education and could reach far more children.

Another question that program directors and coordinators need to consider is the following: How can these programs ensure that the work they do for gifted children *endures*? One way is by doing more for parents. Teachers and administrators often shy away from involving parents because they have a reputation for being "pushy" or demanding. Unfortunately, a few difficult parents can give the whole population a bad name. Because most gifted children live under the care of their parents, I have always felt that programs should include them in the services they offer. These services may include parent seminars, counseling (formal or informal), and regular communications about opportunities and/or sources that could benefit gifted children and their families.

Another way gifted programs can have lasting effect is through career education for gifted students. Often, gifted programming ends with junior high school. In high school, advanced placement classes offered for bright students on the college preparatory track replace what used to be special programs for the gifted. The problem with this is that, although gifted students may have an accelerated and more complex course of study, they lack the opportunity to investigate ideas and possibilities for their future. Instead, they follow the track laid out for them without any time to explore and experiment with career options. A whole other set of issues assails gifted people from high school through college. Some gifted students drop out of college to drift from one thing to the next; others follow a program they think they're supposed to follow (or that a parent wants them to be in), only to change paths several times in the middle of their college years; and still other students refuse to enter college because they feel so fed up with formal schooling they would rather learn in some new context, but they're not sure where or how.

Gifted programs can help gifted young people explore different fields, plan for future development based on their talents and interests, and field-test their choices through internships and/or visits to businesses, courts, museums, labs, universities, nature centers, studios, performing arts rehearsals, and so on. Because of their talents, gifted people look like they know what they're doing. But the appearance of the self-assured gifted young person can be misleading. Inside, that individual may be struggling with some life decisions that require the guidance and support of an older, more experienced person. Parents cannot always perform this task because in many instances, parents find it difficult to separate themselves from their own preconceived ideas about what their children should do.

Gifted programs can make a distinct difference in the lives of many gifted children who become lost or misdirected in their late high school or early college years, when they have to search the deeper, more unpredictable waters of life on their own. By supporting parents and offering career guidance to gifted students, programs can make their contribution a more lasting one. Parents will discover new ways to advocate for their children. On their side, gifted children and young people will find in their programs adults who can help them identify what fields they most enjoy and advise them on the steps they need to take to get where they want to go. Counseling will help talented young people focus on *their own interests*, rather than on what they think those interests should be. Thus, it is highly important that teachers in gifted programs have specific and extensive training in issues relating to giftedness and the problems it raises in children.

Gifted programs are a lot of work and often require great vision and resiliency to sustain. Most of us have developed strong convictions about their potential and long-term value for gifted children, especially in the face of budgetary cuts and the deepening neglect of these students' special needs. When developed and managed properly, gifted programs can create changes that endure beyond the length of a program. Children can begin to take hold of their own talents when they gain confidence in themselves and their own interests. Families can assume a stronger leadership role in advocating for the needs of their children once they understand what practical steps they can take and how to take them.

As researchers and practitioners in the field, we have pooled our insights and experience to create a book that explores how gifted programs work, what they can do for families, and the steps others have taken to develop successful programs in many different environments. The book brings together the ideas of numerous workers in the field of gifted education with many years of experience in programs; it is not ideological, though the authors represent a variety of different viewpoints and backgrounds. Thus, the book should be of use not only to those familiar with all the issues of educational research but also to the nonspecialist parent, teacher, or administrator. Some chapters are more technical than others, but all are accessible to the widest range of individuals who care deeply about gifted children and desire to do more for them.

Gifted children have inherent in them the desire to continually raise their level of giving to the world. We are facilitators of that desire.

*Stand*
*tall*
*and*
*proud.*
*Perhaps*
*I too*
*should be*
*A blade*
*of grass*
*in the sun.*
*You do*
*not belong*
*yet you exist.*

*You and me.*

*The wind*
*bends*
*your back*
*until its will*
*is yours.*
*But you*
*return*
*to stand*
*once more*
*in the shadow*
*Just like*
*I have done.*

—Liliana, Grade 8

# From Needs and Goals to Program Organization

## A Nuts-and-Bolts Guide

*Joan Franklin Smutny*
*Cheryl Lind*

The first day of a gifted program is, perhaps, the most special for those involved in organizing and administering it. After months of planning and preparation, there is nothing quite like seeing hundreds of eager children clutching their schedules and tugging at the hands of their parents. It is at this moment that one most keenly feels that the time and effort involved in producing the program were worthwhile. The children's faces, full of anticipation, are reminders that a number of these children will be experiencing gifted classes for the first time in their lives.

For most of these students, it is rare to have their unique talents, ideas, and interests validated and encouraged by a master teacher or to share their enthusiasm with children like themselves. In a gifted program, these children can invent science experiments, reconstruct mathematical formulas, create poems and stories, participate in theatrical productions, or track the idiosyncratic sightings of UFOs in South America. The exposure to innovative ideas and new fields of knowledge enables gifted students to discover talents they didn't know they had.

Depending on the school district, learning options for gifted students can include pullout programs, differentiated instruction in the classroom, grade skipping, and programs outside regular school hours. In designing and administering summer gifted programs for more than 2,000 students a year, we have become keenly aware of the unique contribution that programs beyond the regular classroom can make in the education of high-ability children. Where else but in a gifted program can a child become a poet, an astronomer, or a detective, composing free verse, exploring new galaxies, or examining the clues in a baffling murder case? Where else can students discover new interests and strengths through course offerings that draw from such a wide range of specializations? Where else can they quickly make friends and enjoy the thrill of working on projects with other children as able and enthusiastic as they?

Our own programs, administered through the Center for Gifted at National-Louis University in Evanston, Illinois, are generally scheduled for 5 days a week in 2- to 3-week sessions through the duration of the summer. We also run 5-week programs on Sunday afternoons during the winter. The sessions run in various locations around the greater Chicago area, and a typical program offers around 15 to 20 classes. Depending on the age level served by the program, classes run for either an hour or 90 minutes, and students attend either two or three classes each day of the program.

We have included this chapter specifically for those of you who desire a practical guide for developing gifted programs. It is only a thumbnail sketch of the many details involved in the organization of such a project. Separate chapters in this book examine some of what is covered here (such as content or assessment) in more depth; this chapter should be read in the context of the book as a whole.

This chapter is *not* a recipe for creating gifted programs; it is a list of necessary ingredients. How these ingredients are combined and in what order and priority are elements that should evolve from the unique circumstances and needs of each community. This chapter focuses on insights learned in the organization and administration of Center for Gifted programs, but we believe the ideas here apply to a much wider variety of program contexts. Many different types of programs are needed to serve the gamut of high-ability children, but all programs involve the following tasks:

1. Reckoning needs and goals

2. Selecting a target population

3. Establishing identification methods

4. Designing and implementing curriculum appropriate for the target population

5. Selecting and developing teachers

6. Hiring administration and support staff

7. Evaluating the program

8. Budgeting and funding

9. Developing a marketing and dissemination plan

10. Developing a timeline for the program

11. Finding sites for the program

12. Planning for the first day: class schedules, attendance, and transportation

## RECKONING OF NEEDS AND GOALS

Itemizing the needs and goals a program will meet is the first step in development. A list of goals will inform the program's administrators of all the organizational decisions they must make in developing the program.

For example, if a program aims to respond to the need for more creative content or for a much broader range of courses, including the arts, then one of the goals must be to establish identification procedures that draw from criteria besides standardized test scores. There is a full educational literature (see, e.g., Gardner, 1993) defending nontraditional criteria, so there should be no embarrassment in taking advantage of it. Similarly, the goal of developing creativity in children demands that teachers must have the qualifications that enable them not only to impart knowledge at an advanced level but also to stimulate original, creative thought in their students, for it is this thought that climbs the steep but imperative mount of applicability. To this end, formal training and experience in the education of the gifted are highly desirable in teachers, though candidates should be evaluated on a case-by-case basis. In some cases, mentoring by an experienced teacher may proxy for formal training for the purposes of the program. Teachers must also have a sophisticated understanding of their subject in order to respond to the many unexpected ideas and solutions that arise from creative children. This combination of teaching qualifications and subject expertise is rare but invaluable to the success of a program.

In developing a list of needs and goals, it is useful to begin with an introspective reckoning. What need, situation, circumstance, or observation stimulated the idea to start a gifted program? What do gifted children most need in the community? Do the services currently available for gifted students meet the expectations of the children, parents, administration, and teachers involved? However the idea came about, everyone involved in the program needs a clear sense of a program's rationale. The planning group will only function properly with a common vision to guide it. Faculty members often use a program's mission as a guiding principle for developing curriculum. One of the first things parents want to know when they inquire about a program is the following: What are the goals and priorities of this particular program, and how are they different from programs offered elsewhere?

Gifted programs generally should aim to meet the needs of three populations—children, parents, and teachers. First and foremost, of course, are the children. After the first session of a program, it is not unusual for parents to tell program administrators about their children's enthusiasm. They often say that on the way home from the program, their children describe, in minute detail, the activities of the classes. They describe the teachers and the other students they enjoyed interacting with that day. This is not surprising because bored and apathetic gifted students come to life in a place where they can participate in projects and activities that challenge their talents and provide new direction, insight, and focus for their interests. Conceptualizing high-ability children's needs for a program must always remain within the framework of activating their enthusiasm.

In formalizing the ways a program can activate enthusiasm among students, it is often valuable to specify the needs met by the program. Here, resource books on gifted education (e.g., Colangelo & Davis, 1991; Gallagher & Gallagher, 1994) and practical advice books for gifted children and their parents (e.g., Alvino, 1985; Galbraith, 1983) may be of great help to the practitioner. The list of needs can extend beyond what is listed below and will vary slightly depending on the format and philosophy of the individual program. Most programs offer the following:

- course subjects and activities that challenge students both academically and creatively;
- content that connects to real conditions, situations, or issues in the world;
- opportunities for intensive focus and exploration in a nonpressurized environment where students can test, experiment, and innovate without having to generate final products or solutions prematurely;
- a learning environment where gifted children can feel nurtured and encouraged and where they can develop a stronger sense of belonging and self-worth;
- a wide selection of courses in math, science, law, economics, social science, language arts, visual art, and performing arts that accommodate a diversity of talent, as well as a diverse student body;

- opportunities to interact and work closely with other gifted students—to share ideas, benefit from others' knowledge, and collaborate on subjects of mutual interest;
- highly qualified teachers—experts in their fields—who can translate their knowledge into stimulating activities and project ideas for gifted students;
- teachers who are empathetic to the emotional and intellectual challenges gifted students often have and are able to encourage and nurture their growth in new areas;
- an emphasis on hands-on activities, experimentation, and creativity that provides an alternative focus and method for all subjects and that encourages independent thinking and risk taking.

Overall, programs should target the need for more divergent thinking activities in all subjects and offer many opportunities for invention and creative expression. Students should apply and experiment with knowledge in all subjects and use a variety of media and materials for their work. Gifted students are not only hungry for more intellectual and creative challenge; they need to *do* things! Therefore, all classes should challenge children to use new learning and skills to experiment, produce, and create.

Gifted programs also serve two other populations—parents and teachers. The knowledge parents have about giftedness varies, but most of them are dissatisfied with their children's schooling and are concerned about their academic, creative, and emotional well-being. They often will tell you that their child is bored, stifled by linear assignments, ostracized by the other kids, or denied access to more challenging or stimulating material. It is highly important to address parents' needs in any program for gifted children. If parents do not understand giftedness or fully comprehend the benefits that can accrue to gifted students by participating in a gifted program, they will lose interest and begin to question whether their children even require special services at all. Parents are typically grateful for any opportunities offered to learn more about giftedness, network with other parents, and feel involved— even welcomed—by teachers. A most useful feature of a gifted program is an "open house" at the end of the program, where parents can visit each class and see the progress their children have made.

Most gifted programs recognize the need to serve children and their parents. There is also, however, another population that should be served by programs—teachers. Teachers should find stimulation and solace in a gifted program. Many teachers enjoy working with talented students and feel frustrated by the limited opportunities available to them in the regular school curriculum. They relish the opportunity to design a more challenging and creative curriculum, to develop materials and activities that stimulate original responses in gifted children. Even teachers who come from walks of life outside education (e.g., practicing scientists, artists, actors, authors, etc.) enjoy a break from their professional lives to work with talented students eager to learn. Gifted students frequently raise interesting questions, pose problems, and bring unique insights that inspire and invigorate teachers.

The program's goals should be communicable in the form of a mission statement or rationale and should be written down on all promotional pieces. The mission statement is the first thing printed on all the flyers the Center for Gifted disseminates. For example, the first paragraph in the flyer for Project—a 3-week intensive summer program for gifted 6th- to 10th-grade students—reads as follows:

> Project 2002 emphasizes creativity and critical thinking while exploring diverse subject matter in a challenging, creative environment, free from the pressure of tests or grades. All activities invite active, hands-on participation, inspire enthusiasm for learning and elicit a desire to expand intellectual and inventive horizons.

Parents and teachers can quickly grasp the program goals and priorities and can see immediately if it matches their interests.

Sometimes simultaneous with the listing of needs and goals is the selection of a target population of gifted students whose needs the program will address.

## SELECTING A TARGET POPULATION

A target population may mean students with high ability in particular areas (such as the sciences or arts), or it may refer to geographic, cultural, or socioeconomic factors. In either case, having a clear sense of the target population at the outset of the planning process will guide coordinators' decisions about identification procedures, curriculum development, faculty searches, and assessment. A program focusing on math and science, for example, will use identification measures that may differ from one that includes all subjects or one that attempts to reach underrepresented gifted students (e.g., bilingual, multicultural, urban, and/or rural poor). Smutny (2002) has discussed alternative identification measures for specific student populations in great detail. The Center for Gifted ran a bilingual gifted program that reevaluated selection procedures; hired bilingual consultants to advise on course content, teaching styles, and activities; and developed projects sensitive to the cultural and linguistic differences of this population. It also involved community aides, bilingual teachers to help in classrooms where gifted students needed extra language support, and a system to keep parents involved and informed.

Targeting a student population can be quite exciting. It allows administrators and teachers to support gifted populations in ways that other programs have not. For example, many programs focus on math and science, but very few are specifically designed for gifted girls and young women.

Many recent studies have shown that girls gifted in math and science turn away from these subjects at more advanced levels, either because of cultural biases or because of the girls' own developmental priorities (Smutny, 1998a). Parents of gifted girls will affirm that this is an area of great need. As program developers take steps to design a program for this target group, they need to reevaluate the standard approach to identification, curriculum development, and the selection of faculty. A program organized to support gifted girls in math and science would be inconsistent if it did not expand identification measures, incorporate more women into the faculty, and redesign teaching materials and strategies to accommodate some of the issues and challenges encountered by this population.

## ESTABLISHING IDENTIFICATION MEASURES

Whatever gifted group is targeted for the program, the goal of supporting that group will direct most of the program's organization. It is vital that the target population determine the selection process. Test scores can sometimes say little—if anything—about a child's creative ability when the child's framework is not the mainstream. Depending on the program's target population, alternative measures of giftedness may be necessary for evaluation.

While being flexible, program planners do need to develop *specific* criteria for admission. Although federal and state guidelines are helpful, they can also be restrictive among some target populations. For example, most schools use standardized testing as an indicator of ability and school performance to measure achievement. These two factors have their usefulness, but gifted students who test poorly and/or underachieve (Baldwin, 2002) will slip through the cracks if these two indicators carry more weight than other methods. In many cases, teacher checklists of behaviors, peer nomination, self-nomination, parent observations, portfolios of student work (at home as well as school), nominations by community leaders and mentors, and informal interviews give a more complete picture of what a child can do and what he or she desires to achieve.

Students in regular schools may have exceptional gifts, but because they perform at an average level in a couple of subjects, they may not receive any support for their talents. In some cases, as discussed in Gallagher and Bristol (1989), a learning disability may cause a student to struggle in certain activities; in other cases, low self-esteem over a number of years can create a self-fulfilling prophecy of average performance in a talented child (LeVine & Kitano, 1998). There are other reasons why gifted students might not be identified. Students who hear gunshots at night in their neighborhoods or who attend schools where the primary focus is maintaining security or getting students to achieve the minimum requirements for promotion to the next grade are highly underrepresented by traditional identification techniques. These students typically have had no exposure to advanced instruction and live in situations where giftedness is an unrecognized quality. They often do not appear gifted to those used to identifying children from more affluent and secure environments. Multiple-criteria approaches to identification help to level entrance requirements for these students.

Program planners need to communicate the criteria they are using to determine eligibility, and ideally, they should provide this information in print so that parents can refer to it when they fill out applications for their children. In the Center for Gifted programs, admission demands evidence of ability, in the form of standardized test scores, grades, or other sources. Parents are often helpful in selecting the most accurate measures. We also require a recommendation by a teacher, counselor, or principal and, for younger children, parental observations of talent, including lists of behaviors, abilities, and tendencies that indicate giftedness. On occasion, giftedness has been established in other ways—through conferencing with parents, conducting director and teacher interviews of the child in question, and/or reviewing portfolios of the child's work.

## DESIGN AND IMPLEMENT CURRICULUM APPROPRIATE FOR THE TARGET POPULATION

The list of needs and goals will again be of highest importance in developing and delivering curriculum for the target population. Unlike a regular school curriculum where little divergence is possible, the program's curriculum can focus on subjects rarely explored in the classroom—for example, architecture, archaeology, or poetry. Unmet needs of students, parents, and teachers can be most directly met through curriculum design and implementation.

Teachers must have a clear sense of the needs and goals the program is intended to meet. Then, they can develop the concepts or theories to be communicated and, from that basis, design and implement a series of activities and projects that encourage both critical and creative thinking (i.e., analytical and synthetic thinking in nonlinear, imaginative ways) on Type II and Type III levels (Renzulli & Reis, 1986).

In-class projects should become progressively more complex as students become more adept at tackling advanced concepts. Far from being an unstructured element of curriculum, creativity should be one that provides the most challenge (Torrance, Murdock, & Fletcher, 1996). Creativity demands not only a mastery of subject matter but also flexibility of thought in applying known strategies to new situations. Teachers may find practical subject-specific guidelines to appropriate gifted curriculum development for young children in Smutny, Walker, and Meckstroth (1997); for mathematics in Freeman (2001); and for preteen and teenage students in Drake (1998).

Moving from curricular design to implementation involves creativity and imagination. The following are some useful general guidelines for curriculum design in gifted programs, along with a sampling of some Center for Gifted courses and descriptions from our catalogue illustrating them. These should give an idea of how implementation should follow from design, although obviously, the courses any program offers will depend on the target population served.

- Select a topic or focus within a field that is conceptually or theoretically interesting to a sizable population of students and one that is narrow enough to thoroughly explore during the duration of the program.

> *The Science of Flight.* Challenge current scientific theories about why things fly. Study, design, and construct a variety of aircraft and try to fly them. Endeavor to defy concepts developed by Venturi, Galileo, von Braun, Bell, Goddard, the Bernoullis, and others as you create helicopters, straw flyers, balloon jets, water rockets, Nerf ball cannons, and tetrahedra kites in pursuit of perfect flight (Grades 6-10).

- Design a series of activities that follow a conceptual, theoretical, or creative progression and lead students from one project/activity to the next.

> *Tall Tales, Small Tales, Fairy Tales.* Imagine, create, and dramatize your way around, through, over, and under wild things and crazy places in literature (Grades K-1).

- Include projects that actively draw from the skills, concepts, discoveries, innovations, discussions, and research undertaken by the students and the teacher.

> *Defying Laws of Physics.* Challenge traditional theorems (after all, they're only *assumed* to be true!) as you forge into the facts and fables of sound, pressure, light, heat, and electricity (Grades 5-6).

- Incorporate creativity, imagination, innovation, and invention (consider how critical and creative thinking can be integrated with more interesting results and how the subject at hand can be presented to allow for greater variations in approach and execution).

> *Becoming an Architect.* Perform daring feats of engineering as you explore the art and science of building design and construction; probe the structural equipoise of strength, practicality, and aesthetics; draft scale drawings; and build your own creative models (Grades 4-7).

- Develop the class sessions to allow for differences in education, experience, and ability.

*The Artist's Studio.* Explore various methods and muses, including sculpture, weaving, batik, and printmaking; then create your own masterpieces in this multimedia workshop (Grades 4-7).

- Provide a bounty of materials for classroom use. The catalysts (initial activities, supplies, media, magazines, books, computer programs, audio and visual sources, etc.) play a crucial role in stimulating original thought.

*Filmmaking.* Explore scientific mechanisms of the projector and camera. Critique short films and create your own camera-less film using original media. Discover the Bolex camera, light meter, and projector; build sets; write scripts; and invent, create, and manipulate characters to produce your own animated film (Grades 6-10).

Involving faculty in the development of curriculum for the program is often a useful tactic. Once newly hired teachers understand the objectives of the program, they typically have their own ideas about topics that might be integrated into the curriculum. Consult often with program teachers to ensure that the activities provide the conceptual and practical challenges gifted students need. Of course, this type of teacher-administration interaction is best when faculty have been selected with care to meet the needs and goals of the program.

## SELECTING AND DEVELOPING TEACHERS

A gifted program is only as good as its faculty. Ideally, instructors should have not only expertise in their subject but also an ability to translate it into activities where students can express their understanding in creative, original applications. Teachers should be selected based on criteria that include the following:

- Advanced knowledge of theory and application in a subject
- Ability to translate sophisticated material into stimulating and challenging projects for gifted students of different levels
- Ability to provide a variety of hands-on, experimental activities
- Specific training in theories of different learning styles and an ability to modify curricula and activities to suit the preferred learning styles of individual children
- Warm disposition, empathy for the feelings and experiences of gifted children, and an ability to respond sensitively to their unique emotional and cognitive needs
- Understanding of giftedness and an ability to establish an open and nurturing classroom atmosphere conducive to bold experiments and risk-taking endeavors

One should not necessarily turn away prospective teachers with little classroom experience if they have other important qualifications (such as expertise in their field and an understanding of application, theory, and concept) and if they have inspired ideas about what they want to accomplish with gifted students. Instead, it may be possible to arrange for them to visit a program already running or, if this is not possible, to provide them with special assistance and support during their initial meetings with the children. They may also benefit from "on-the-job training" or mentoring, working with an experienced teacher to learn ways of communicating their knowledge to students. The Center for Gifted has had as many professional nonteachers in our programs as regular classroom or private school teachers, and both have provided exceptional instruction for gifted students.

Preparing teachers for a program is critical. A new teacher needs to understand the philosophy and goals of the program, the level and type of ability they will most likely find among gifted students at the grade level they are teaching, the unique problems and issues gifted children in the target population face, and the importance of integrating different learning styles into projects and activities.

Once program administrators have hired the faculty, they also need to provide ongoing support and assistance. This ensures that all the teachers understand the aims of the program while still allowing latitude for individual teaching styles and approaches to course content. One way to accomplish this is by beginning each program with a faculty meeting and then having regular follow-up sessions so that teachers can ask questions and network with each other on issues relating to the target population, parents, and administrators. The director and administrators should also keep track of how students are responding to the activities and assignments provided by teachers and make themselves available to the instructors for additional advice if they so desire. It is critical to support teachers, some of whom, if they have not had a great deal of experience in working with gifted students, may find working with them more difficult than they imagined. When they feel free to express their concerns or frustrations, they can find solutions to their teaching problems.

Finding creative teachers with expertise in a variety of fields can be challenging. It is worthwhile to consider schools for the gifted and private schools, where faculty are experienced in gifted education; universities; master's degree programs in gifted education; technology firms and science institutes that are invested in helping talented students; and art, dance, and theater studios. Many of the best teachers will come from referrals by parents and other teachers, so it is worthwhile to involve these groups in the faculty selection process. Signs in university departments, student lounges of education colleges where gifted specialists may be, public libraries, and art studios can also bring in good applicants.

## COMMUNICATING WITH PARENTS

Gifted programs need some form of outreach to parents in order to create a foundation that lasts. Parents have a critical role to play in the development and success of gifted programs. They have a mine of information about their children's abilities—the different projects the children have done in school and at home, their hobbies and tastes, and the many behaviors parents have observed firsthand since their children were born. Teachers should write an introductory letter to parents at the beginning of the program that describes the class and the kinds of projects the children will undertake.

Some teachers go farther and ask parents for specific information on the children's strengths, abilities, and learning preferences. They may also ask for parent participation. This could include helping to make costumes, providing materials for a writing class, doing a short presentation in a law class, lending a video that applies to an entomology class, and so on. Not all instructors need go this far, but they should always make themselves available to those parents who have questions or concerns about their children.

Parents who bring their children to gifted programs will usually take advantage of all the resources available. At the Center for Gifted, parent workshops are given while children are in classes. Speakers at the workshops focus on a variety of issues of interest to the gifted community, providing sources and materials for parents to take home and creating a forum for them to network with each other. These seminars have proven effective in helping parents understand the importance of special education for gifted students and of parent advocacy as a means of creating more opportunity for their children. Through the seminars, parents meet others facing similar problems and gain new insights and knowledge they can use with their own children.

Another opportunity for parent outreach, mentioned earlier, is an "open house" during or after the last session of a program. Performance classes often have productions to showcase; art students can display their sculptures, paintings, or collages; writing students can share their poems and stories; science students can demonstrate their experiments or inventions; and math students can display geometric structures they have constructed or explain formulas they have learned in a variety of contexts. Open-house sessions are culminating experiences for both parents and children to see how far they have progressed during the course of the program. They help parents and students recognize the value of the program and encourage them to return.

## HIRING ADMINISTRATION AND SUPPORT STAFF

Most programs cannot afford to hire a great number of administrators, but it is possible for a few dedicated individuals to wear several hats. Basic and necessary administrative and staff positions include the following:

- Program director/codirectors
- Budget director (administering payroll, expenses, reimbursements for supplies, etc.)
- Site coordinators if more than one program is operating simultaneously (these tend to be temporary positions)
- Administrative assistants to handle marketing (working with directors to design flyers, generating school lists for dissemination of flyers, keeping track of students enrolled in previous programs), process student applications, locate and rent space for classrooms, schedule students into classes, respond to parent inquiries and concerns, and send assessment forms to parents and teachers

There is no way to predict precisely how many staff members will be needed in advance. Estimates of staff requirements depend on the size of the program, the availability of funding, and the multitasking talents (giftedness!) of potential staff members. Due to funding difficulties, most programs begin with very few staff members, though these are typically foot soldiers for the gifted education movement who are willing to contribute extra time and effort to make the program run.

The most practical way to go about staffing is to determine all the areas that need managing and then to consider which areas are already covered and which require additional staff. If the program belongs to an institute, university, or school, new positions will be proposed formally. Having a job description available and a clear rationale for the creation of the new position will often streamline this process. If funding for additional staff is not available, consider the recruitment of parent volunteers. In our programs and others we have observed, parents who have extra time and those with areas of special expertise are often quite willing to devote time to a cause that directly benefits their children. Contracting with the parent for help with the program in exchange for reduced tuition will eliminate the need to pay some staff directly out of pocket.

## EVALUATING THE PROGRAM

Evaluation is something almost everyone would like to avoid. For some, it seems like a cumbersome process of gathering assessments from different constituencies, all of whom have something to criticize. Far from being a compendium of complaints, however, evaluation can actually be a powerful catalyst for growth. Without it, a program would move blindly into the future without any sense of how it is benefiting students and without any impetus for growth and expansion. Gifted programs without any form of evaluation put themselves at risk. As Dettmer (1985) observed, "Because gifted programs are not popular and probably never will be, they must be defended and promoted by solid evidence of gifted student growth, cost effectiveness of the program and positive ripple effects for all students throughout the school system" (p. 146).

Before designing a structure for evaluation, program founders need to ask themselves, Who needs to know what (Clark, 1988)? That is, what do parents, students, researchers, program administrators, and school districts need to know about the performance of the program? Parents, for example, will want to know more about the kinds of activities their children did in an advanced math class, and they will likely want to know this *before* the program is over. A program director will want to know exactly which classes and activities worked and didn't work for the participating children. A teacher will want to know which projects the students found most challenging and why. To determine how a program is performing, all participants need an opportunity to express themselves at the end of the program. A comprehensive evaluation should assess students' academic and creative progress, social growth, decision-making skills, and leadership abilities, as well as program and teacher effectiveness.

*Student Evaluations.* Teachers should evaluate each student individually at the end of the program. Parents of gifted children want to know more than the number or letter grades they are used to getting from the schools. Each teacher may be allowed to create his or her own form for evaluation, but it should include the following components:

- introductory paragraphs about the activities in class and the teacher's impressions about how the students responded and grew over the length of the program;
- a grid to rank student performance on general areas of intellectual and/or creative ability as well as attitude and application;
- follow-up comments that specifically address the child's particular talents, growth, and progress; and
- areas where the teacher sees a need for more work.

The evaluation may then go both to the student's home for the parents to see and to the child's school. In this way, parents gain insight from the teacher's perspective about their child's ability to do high-level work, and the school also has a record on file. This is critical evidence of talent, particularly in cases when the gifted student attends a school where no gifted education exists or when the student has been underestimated or ignored.

*Program Evaluations.* Parents and their children should receive an evaluation form at the end of the program on which they can confer and respond to key questions about the classes and program performance. These forms can also be mailed to parents when the student evaluations are sent out. With help from their children, parents can describe which classes their children preferred and why, which activities they found most interesting and challenging, and what aspects of the program they liked best. Did the children feel affirmed, encouraged to try new things, and excited about what they were learning? They should also be allowed to identify what did *not* work—which classes proved disappointing and why; aspects of the curriculum that seemed redundant, obscure, or confusing; and problems that persisted through the length of the program. This information is extremely important both for the teachers and for administrators who must hold themselves responsible for the program's effectiveness. It is common for some students to discover that they do not like particular courses after all—or for a particular teacher and student to be ill matched. But when many students complain about the same class, administrators need to inquire more deeply, confer with the teacher, and take concrete steps to rectify the situation. In some cases, this may mean finding a new instructor for that particular class.

Evaluation should be ongoing, not merely confined to the end of the program. The more administrators know about the program *as it is in progress*, the more they can head off potential problems before they become significant. There are some simple ways to do this. One is for administrators to take time during the program to unobtrusively observe classes. Another is for administrators to make themselves available to teachers for assistance and support on a daily basis. All of this must be done sensitively, though. From the first meeting with teachers, it is best to create an open and nurturing environment for them—an atmosphere where they feel free to share how their classes are progressing. This is vital to the process of ongoing evaluation. If teachers feel nervous about their performance and cover up the areas where they feel unsure of their work, they will keep their thoughts to themselves and not seek the support they need. Also, classroom observation of fearful teachers will become unwelcome and may interfere with the normal teacher-student interaction.

The other dimension of ongoing evaluation we have found particularly helpful is regular staff meetings. Teachers have a great deal of data at their fingertips simply by their interactions with students, parents, and the administration every day. They can assess both students and the program. Staff meetings prove effective in providing a forum for teachers to share common issues that arise in a classroom full of active, highly intense gifted students. They also allow teachers to provide informal assessments on a variety of subjects. New teachers gain inspiration and encouragement by sharing with those who have had more experience in gifted programs. Regular meetings also enable administrators to communicate any issues or needs that arise and assess how the program's classes are progressing from week to week.

All of this information will help program administrators to see what worked well and where the weak points are. It is wise to not allow a few sour comments to become distractive to the evaluation process. Some parents, teachers, and even kids seem determined never to be satisfied. A few angry people with chips on their shoulders should not be allowed to make the administrators feel the program failed to do what it set out to do. It is best to keep in mind the broader picture. How did most of the children respond? How did most of the participating families feel about their experience? Gifted programs need a great deal of nurturing, especially in the beginning. The assessments should be used to explore how what is working well can be strengthened and what can be done to help the program grow and expand for the next session.

Chapter 13 in this volume will also be of help in formulating assessment techniques.

## BUDGETING AND FUNDING

Budgets for gifted programs depend on the organizations that support them, as well as on the policies of the funding sources. Programs run by a small group of parents and teachers may not have a budget at all when they start out, relying exclusively on tuition to reimburse the costs. Whatever the situation, it is necessary to plan the size and scope of a program within budgetary limits. It is also highly desirable, however, to be always seeking new sources for expansions to the program.

There is no way to tell what any particular gifted program will cost without knowing the specific details about it. Teacher salaries and the cost of renting sites (often schools) vary from one geographic location to the next. Nevertheless, an approach to the planning of a first-time budget might involve the following steps.

- Start small. Gifted programs are always costlier than expected. Plan for the number of children you can handle given your present resources.
- Write down all costs—personnel and nonpersonnel. Are there any areas where costs could be significantly reduced? An example might be a program run by a committed group who agree to teach without salaries for the first program or for significantly reduced salaries. Another example might be supplies that can be provided by a school, institute, or university or by staff and volunteers.
- Pad estimates of each cost on the list by 10%. As already mentioned, expenses usually exceed expectations.
- Create a timeline for the disbursement of expenses. Again, depending on the program's situation and organization, various types of paperwork may need to be completed by a deadline.

Many programs can function reasonably well from the resources of their organization and tuition. However, at some point, it may be desirable to expand the program. For example, when we decided to make a special effort to include urban and minority gifted students for a 3-week summer program in the Chicago area, we applied for special funds to cover 60 scholarships, plus the extra costs of daily bus transport and additional faculty members. Most foundations do not give money to individuals or groups of individuals. This has been a strong incentive for smaller groups of committed parents and teachers to create nonprofit organizations.

Nonprofit organizations can take several practical steps to apply for funds.

• Contact a local organization for grant makers. In Chicago, the Donor's Forum serves this purpose. Two useful Web sites that will be helpful in finding such local associations are the List of Regional Associations of Grant Makers (www.indoors.com/RAGlist.html) and Foundation Center—Links to Philanthropic Resources (fdncenter.org/onlib/npr-links/npr05.html). The organizations listed on these sites provide guidance in grant writing and can help locate potential donors in your area.

• Once a list of potential foundations and/or businesses has been found, contact them for applications and ask for deadline dates. Put these dates on your calendar.

• Have the specific project or plan clearly formulated as you write your proposal. Most foundations do not want their funds used for regular operating costs, as they are not interested in supporting an organization that is struggling to keep its head above water—no matter how worthy the cause! In the proposal mentioned earlier, we focused on the request to support minority and urban gifted children who had little or no resources available to them in their communities.

• Formulate a strong rationale for the project—one that demonstrates real need and that clearly explains how the program can fulfill that need in a way that other organizations do not or cannot.

• Create a budget that itemizes all costs—personnel and nonpersonnel—for the specific project needing support. Most application guidelines also request the complete budget for the program to verify fiscal soundness.

• Show the proposal to others; if possible, work with a grant maker's organization for advice and assistance.

## DEVELOPING A MARKETING AND DISSEMINATION PLAN

Marketing a program begins with the families and children the founders know personally. The program's teachers can contact parents, other teachers, and the gifted children they teach in their regular classrooms, explaining how the program will operate and asking if they might be interested. It is especially desirable to discuss a proposed program with parents—get them involved! Encourage them to talk with other parents and hold a series of meetings to discuss the program.

In a university, a program founder can make use of speaking engagements at schools, conferences, and parent groups as opportunities to talk about a new program. Schools where workshops have been given can be contacted and asked if they would be willing to disseminate flyers. Informational meetings can be held in local school districts.

For groups of local parents and teachers, word of the program can be spread most easily through the schools where their own children are or where they themselves teach. Principals or superintendents can be contacted, and a meeting with the group can be arranged to discuss the program and the role that local schools might play. Local libraries can be contacted for permission to use space for some speakers on gifted education who can inform local communities about the special challenges faced by gifted students in the regular schools. Gifted coordinators from surrounding districts should be asked if they would be willing to disburse flyers to their gifted students.

Marketing a new program takes time. A program should begin marketing at least two seasons before it starts. In the winter months, for example, it would be appropriate to begin advertising summer programs. At the end of summer, flyers for winter programs can go out. Once an organization has run several programs, lists of former participants can be used for future mailings on upcoming programs. Enthusiastic customers usually come back and often bring others with them. For our programs, we do a mass mailing to all the schools near the sites where we hold programs. We also distribute flyers whenever we give talks, do workshops in the local schools, or teach graduate courses on gifted education. Teachers can also be persuasive voices for gifted children in their own districts.

Spreading the word about gifted programs should have a personal touch. It is not enough to simply send informational materials to a school. In fact, more often than not, information sent in this way does not end up in teachers' mailboxes. Anyone who has worked in a school knows that school administrators do not see the distribution of mass mailings as a priority. Similarly, a family may receive a flyer in the mail and lose it a day later under a pile of newspapers. About 3 months before the programs begin and after information has gone out by mail, it is helpful to get a pool of people together to make phone calls. They can contact parents to ask if they have received the flyers, if they have any questions, and if they think their child might be interested in attending the program. Often, parents are interested but misplaced the flyer, had questions but didn't get around to calling, or were confused about the dates. Schools can be called after flyers are sent out to check on their status. Did they receive them? Have they been distributed? Are there any questions or concerns? This kind of contact—made in a friendly, low-key way—has resulted in much greater participation in our programs than we would ever have had otherwise. When a program still has room for a few more students, staff members can tell people interested in the program that there are extra spaces if they know any other gifted children who might be interested. It is not uncommon for parents inquiring about the program to ask for extra flyers so that they can share the information with other families. Gifted programs are less institutions than networks, and like all networks, the benefit any single child receives from the program is increased by the presence of familiar peers. People in the gifted community—whether they be parents, teachers, kids, administrators, or counselors—tend to know each other and often move as a unit.

Whatever form of marketing a program may choose—mailings, phone contacts, informal talks at the local library or school, advertising, or any combination of these—start early! Six months ahead of the program's first day is not too soon.

## DEVELOPING A TIMELINE FOR THE PROGRAM

After a program is completed the first time, it will be easier to grasp the time the process takes for the next program. Some points to keep in mind in developing a timeline include the following:

- Begin marketing right away—6 months in advance, if possible. Create a promo piece (such as a flyer) that can be used for mailings or for any situation of contact with parents or teachers. The promo piece can be used like a business card.

- Teachers need time to get acquainted with the program. Some professionals may have had very little teaching experience—in which case, they may require more preparation and support than regular classroom teachers. Unless it is an emergency, it is best to avoid hiring teachers just before the program begins.

- Renting space in the summer is typically much more difficult than during the school year. Start looking *early*. As soon as the geographical area for a gifted program is decided on, start looking for space right away. Be sure to think through the program's needs—computers, art supplies, science labs, and other facilities. A great number of schools undergo renovations in the summer months and do not allow any part of the building to be rented. A situation in which students and teachers are ready to begin the program but have nowhere to go should be avoided at all costs.

- Keeping the running schedule of deadlines for foundational funding up-to-date is highly important. Once one good proposal has been written, its content can be modified to address the priorities and goals of other foundations.

- Mailings of promotional materials must be sent out early—especially for summer programs. Schools have many other pressing priorities after spring break, such as graduation and end-of-the-year testing, and it is difficult for a program to compete with these in the minds of teachers and school administrators. The same rule applies in mailings to parents. Families begin summer plans quite early. If the information reaches them by early spring and then the program follows up with a phone call, there will be a far better chance of interesting them in the program.

- For programs developed within organizations, it is best to find out how much time paperwork will take to be processed before the program preparations begin. Delays can easily occur in administrative bureaucracy. Most organizations have monthly deadlines for expense reports, teacher salaries, and approvals of various sorts. Getting this information in advance will eliminate the need to plead with various departmental bureaucrats later when time is running short.

## FINDING SITES FOR THE PROGRAM

Programs meet in different kinds of places depending on the organization or group sponsoring them. For afterschool or in-school programs, the school's facilities can typically be used. At a university or for an independent group of parents and teachers, a site convenient to the student applicants must be found. In our summer programs, we use approximately 10 sites across different geographical areas of Chicago. We typically look for schools to rent because the size of each program (approximately 250 students) requires a large number of classrooms, including computer rooms, science labs, art rooms, and stages. For smaller programs, however, be creative! Studios, learning centers, museums, or even large houses may meet your needs.

If a program includes science, art, or any kind of performance class, the focus should primarily be on schools. Some space may be available in a community center or YMCA, but this will generally be limited. Most community centers have activities throughout the year and rarely have the equipment necessary for a gifted program. In looking for schools, explore first those schools with which program administrators or teachers have connections—either through a contact or a workshop given there or through a parent group. Independent schools should also be included in the search. They often most appreciate receiving the extra funds, and because they are not solely state funded, administrators have an incentive to seek further means, especially during the summer months when the school would otherwise sit idle. Renting a site will require a contract agreement. Charges for space vary, so researching and comparing prices will often be productive. Some districts provide discount site rentals to groups that hire some of the district's own staff and students, so faculty hiring should be considered in conjunction with site location.

## PLANNING FOR THE FIRST DAY: CLASS SCHEDULES, ATTENDANCE, AND TRANSPORTATION

By the first day of the program, each child needs a schedule of classes. In our programs, children choose five classes in order of preference on their applications. They actually attend only three classes, but a list of five means that if their first choice is filled, their preferences will be respected for alternatives. It is important to keep track of applications as they arrive. For a large program or one in which certain classes are quite popular, the principle of first-come, first-serve may be the fairest allocation mechanism. Computer classes tend to fill up quickly. When classes fill up, a note to that effect on any additional flyers sent out will avoid confusion and frustration between parents and program staff.

Class choices can become complicated and messy if policies are not clear from the very beginning. Decisions to be made for each program include the following:

• How are spaces in popular classes to be allocated? As already mentioned, first-come, first-serve may be best, but other allocation schemes may also be effective. Giving each student his or her first-choice class before assigning other classes on a first-come, first-served basis, instead of assigning all classes by date of application, is another method.

• Can children change classes, and if so, when should the deadline for this be? It is preferable for gifted children to have the option of changing classes if a class turns out to be different from what they expected, but this choice should be made within the first few classes to be fair to teachers and other students.

• How late in a program can a new child join? The student needs to be able to catch up with the other children and participate fully. If a program is 10 weeks, it would be difficult to accept new students after the third week.

Each faculty member must keep attendance, which includes keeping accurate records of new students and/or any changes that occur during the first few sessions. Each child needs to be kept track of at all times for the security of the students and the sanity of the parents. Also, teachers can use the attendance list to make notes on each child, so that at the end of the program, they can write detailed evaluations and comments on the students' performance during the course.

Transportation to and from the program is another detail that needs to be prearranged by the time the first day arrives. Some small, local programs may not require special transportation arrangements. Parents can bring their children in their own cars and pick them up later. In other cases, a busing service may be necessary.

It is important to research local bus services before signing a contract with one and to do this research well in advance of the program. Schools and community programs that use buses can give references for reputable and reliable bus services. Regular inquiries from parents about carpooling should also be expected. If a number of applicants wish to carpool, a system to efficiently locate them by geographical area should be created for convenience. The time taken to administer such a system will easily pay for itself in reduced busing costs. Carpooling allows a group of parents to share the burden of transporting children to and from the program and is also a wonderful way for families with gifted children to become acquainted.

## A FINAL NOTE

More than an educational alternative, a gifted program is a community and a culture. When a child walks through the door to find her first class, she becomes part of a small but vibrant world that embraces and inspires her beyond what school has ever done. She can no longer slump at the back of the class or surreptitiously read a book while the class goes over an assignment too easy for her to think about any longer. A gifted child soon realizes this is a different place. Other children seem more like her. The teacher doesn't mind if she comes up with an unconventional, slightly bizarre response. In the halls, kids are streaming in and out of classrooms chatting energetically, and when she peeps into some of the rooms, she sees half-finished art projects, geometric structures in various stages of completion with scribbles and diagrams all over the boards, paintings and photographs to inspire the poems and short stories that now lie piled on the teacher's desk, and, in almost every room, tables crammed with materials that make her want to join in.

Gifted programs can turn the tide for a gifted child who has given up, who no longer expects to learn anything new or interesting, who has begun to believe that he will never fit in with a group of fellow learners, or who wonders if life will simply continue to be an endless round of repetition and routine. Gifted programs can take students along paths they may never travel in a school context and can turn them loose in ways that help them to take greater risks and respond more creatively to a new challenge.

Becoming an inventor, a judge, an aviator, a physicist, a writer, or an artist for the duration of the program places the gifted child in a new universe and enables that individual—perhaps for the first time—to be struck with wonder at the vision.

For these benefits to accrue to gifted youth, however, a program must be well administered, expertly taught, and effectively monitored and evaluated. The rough guidelines presented in this chapter should be helpful in organizing the needs and goals of any program and meeting them through an effectively developed and efficiently run program. The other chapters in this book detail how these guidelines have been successfully implemented in a variety of settings, but each program, like each eager attending child, is unique and deserves special care.

# 2

# Developing and Designing Programs Serving Young Gifted Children

*Joan Franklin Smutny*

*We first noticed Elizabeth was unusual at age 2 when, upon hearing Copland's Rodeo on TV used in an ad, she identified the title and composer after hearing it for the second time. Elizabeth, now age 6, does fifth-grade reading. She writes great poetry and creates her own experiments and math problems.*

*As a toddler, our son had an incredible curiosity about fans. This expanded to furnaces and air conditioning. He inspected every 'unit' within a five-block radius! Once he felt satisfied—years and years later—he expanded his interest to include anatomy and space as well as music.*

These quotes come from parents I have met through the gifted programs I administer at the Center for Gifted at National-Louis University. They illustrate the importance of parent identification in designing programs for young gifted children (age 4 through Grade 2). They also suggest that in many school districts across the nation, young gifted children have a long wait from the day they enter school to the day they are eligible for special instruction.

Though some states include younger students in programming for the gifted, many do not. There is a great need, however, for early identification and intervention in all regions. Gifted children can develop negative thought patterns and work habits in a classroom that offers little stimulation or challenge (Smutny, Walker, & Meckstrom, 1997, p. 6). Support services for the gifted, however, can promote enormous growth in these children. For instance, a child with a keen interest in technology can find a niche for his talents and interests in a gifted program that gives young children an environment to explore science at a more advanced level.

# IDENTIFYING YOUNG CHILDREN FOR GIFTED PROGRAMS

Program developers need to carefully examine the question of identification when dealing with young gifted children. In any student population, homogeneity of talent rarely exists. In the kindergarten through third-grade classroom, the variance in talent among gifted children increases considerably. Physical, social, and cognitive development is rapid and uneven in young gifted children. Cognitive and motor skills come suddenly: One moment the skill is not observable; then it appears. A student who has struggled to read school-assigned texts may catch up and surpass classmates who had helped him previously, or a kindergarten child who reads fourth-grade books may only have mastered spelling and handwriting at the level of those at the lower end of the class. A highly creative child may feel absolutely lost in the simplest math problems because he thinks so differently from what the assignment demands. This young student may show flashes of true talent but may seem so inconsistent that he rarely gets an opportunity to develop his gifts.

For these reasons, the use of one method of identification generally yields few results in the young gifted population (Gross, 1999). Testing may work at one time and not at another; observations may yield insights into one child's language ability, but for another, a highly imaginative story told to peers during a free play period at school may be what reveals that child's talent and imagination. Programs for young talented children need to be sensitive to the inconsistencies that often occur in their performance.

# PARENT INPUT

Parents are often the first to notice the unusual qualities of their gifted young children. They are their children's most accurate judge and are in a unique position to observe talent in a variety of settings and over long periods of time (Louis & Lewis, 1992). A mother may catch her 5-year-old son humming a complete aria on key from the Three Tenors performance on television or reading most of the words from several library books she had read to him several days before. A mother once informed a gifted teacher that her 6-year-old daughter surprised her one day by drawing a picture of the world, including Africa, Asia, and the Americas in considerable detail. She had mastered all the basic shapes, placed them in the correct places on the map, and identified them in her own handwriting. The mother said that all of this took place without her kindergarten teacher or anyone in the family teaching her geography. These examples illustrate why parents should always be included in the identification process—they can provide useful information unavailable from any other source.

My own programs for gifted children in kindergarten through third grade, administered through the Center for Gifted at National-Louis University in Evanston, Illinois, are generally scheduled for 5 days a week in several 2-week sessions throughout the summer. We also run 5-week programs on Sunday afternoons during the winter. The sessions run in various locations throughout the greater Chicago area, and a typical program allows students to choose from 15 or more classes. Each class runs for 50 minutes, and students attend 3 classes each day of the program.

In these programs, we do not require standardized testing for young gifted children to apply, although when tested, most of our students rank above the 95th percentile at national or local norms in at least one subject. Applicants *are* required to provide teacher recommendations assessing special gifts, abilities, achievements, exceptional characteristics, and any other evidence of talent that may be appropriate. I also encourage parents to confer with me or another administrator if they have any questions or concerns; exceptions have been made for children who perform poorly on tests and in school but who are clearly gifted by other measures. For young children, especially ages 4 through 6, parent observation may be the most reliable standard. On the flyer advertising the program to parents, a list of behaviors and abilities considered signs of giftedness in primary students is a helpful aid to parents. Behaviors from various intelligences and common sensitivities are also appropriate to include. Such a list might include the following:

- Has a long attention span for activities that interest him or her
- Works independently and uses initiative
- Loves books and reading activities
- Is extremely curious about many things—asks, "Why? How? What if?"
- Raises insightful questions about abstract ideas such as love, justice, and so on
- Discusses and elaborates on ideas in complex, unusual ways
- Is very interested in causal relationships

- Loves playing with number concepts and figuring out how to solve math problems in unique ways
- Learns quickly and applies knowledge to new contexts with ease
- Has a vivid imagination and an ability to improvise games or toys from commonplace materials; can generate other options for doing something in the spur of the moment
- Is extremely creative—makes up elaborate stories, excuses; sees many possible answers/solutions; spends free time drawing, painting, writing, building, experimenting, and inventing
- Has spontaneous and whimsical sense of humor
- Likes to play with words and absorbs the speech patterns and vocabulary of different people, imitating them in stories, rhythms, and games
- Is often singing, moving rhythmically, or using mime in self-expression
- Is responsive to music and can improvise with easily memorized tunes, rhythms, or sounds
- Is a leader in organizing games and resolving disputes
- Is sensitive to the feelings of others and/or empathic in response to others' sorrows or troubles
- Expresses concern about world problems such as near extinction of animal species, political injustice, poverty, and so on
- Has a high intuitive gift and a willingness to follow "hunches" even if he or she cannot justify them at the moment they come

Parents may have portfolios of their children's talents to show as evidence or to describe in their recommendations—artwork, inventions, experiments, stories, improvised toys, books read, and videos of performances. Most parents are not inclined to overestimate their child's talents and, in fact, many underestimate them significantly. Those few who do initially overestimate their children quickly find that gifted programs are not worth the time or expense when their children benefit little from curriculum not designed for them.

Portfolios provide authentic assessment (see Kingore, 1995). Gathering evidence from a variety of sources (parents, portfolios, teacher observations) will reveal gifted children more effectively.

## TEACHER RECOMMENDATIONS

Parents of gifted students who do not perform well in school or on standardized tests may express nervousness about trying to find someone to recommend their children. This may be particularly acute in situations involving young gifted children because to a much greater degree, it is the parents who must speak for their children instead of the children asking for a recommendation themselves. This situation is common in communities—especially less affluent ones—where giftedness is a low priority because of other pressing needs and problems in the local school district. It is also common when a child's talent is more elusive and difficult for teachers and parents to recognize readily. A parent may say, "Most of the time my child seems just average, but then he will surprise me by coming up with solutions to complex family problems or by fixing my bicycle, which I have struggled to fix myself for weeks, or by asking some rather analytical questions about a political debate."

In this situation, directors of gifted programs may be called on to provide guidance to parents on how to look for talent, especially in those children whose gifts seem inconsistent. They may need to explain how culture, language, learning preferences, or the uneven development of a young child may create misleading impressions. They could discuss the potentially gifted child's creative use of language, level of questioning, problem-solving strategies, depth of knowledge on select subjects, creativity (including improvisational ability, expressive speech, dramatic talent), absorption in a task, deep interest in existential and/or spiritual questions, self-evaluation, preference for novelty or complexity, and ability to synthesize, interpret, and imagine. The list of gifted behaviors should include those associated with a wide range of talents and abilities (creative and academic) and should correspond with actual course content in the program. The list assures parents that giftedness includes more than test scores, encourages them to pursue teacher recommendations more vigorously, and indicates that the program has something specific to offer to their child's strengths and abilities. If parents cannot find a teacher to recommend their child, an informal interview with the parent and child may be in order. Other possibilities include references from a special instructor in a subject of particular interest to the child (e.g., art, music, dance, ecology, computers, etc.), a director of a club or program who supervised a project or some activities that involved the child, or a community person who has witnessed and can attest to the child's special talents.

## DESIGNING CURRICULUM
## FOR YOUNG GIFTED STUDENTS

*Educational Needs.* Deciding on the needs that a program should address is half the job of planning curriculum. Some planning committees or directors may choose to focus on a particular subject area (e.g., the arts or sciences), whereas others may decide to have a broad range of course offerings. Even in the latter case, however, the planners—whoever they may be—need to have a definite philosophy about the educational needs of young gifted students and a clear sense of program objectives (Cohen & Jipson, 1998, p. 398). In general, programs for young children should be broad in terms of the subject areas covered. But all subjects—from science and math to the arts—should emphasize creativity and imagination as essential features of gifted programming for young children.

Research on child development has provided a great deal of information on how young children learn. During the toddler years, exploration is the primary means for discovery and learning; they finger, touch, taste, and shape whatever they can get their hands on. This explorative behavior gradually extends to testing and experimenting with materials at hand to understand how they work and what can be done with them. As higher level thinking advances even further, young primary students engage in constructive behavior (Belgrad, 1998, p. 373), where they create and improvise with these materials to invent things from their own imagination.

In a gifted program, curriculum should not only stimulate and interest young talented children but also expand their critical and creative thinking to new levels. Teachers play a key role in exposing children to the materials that will help them engage new ideas—experiment with and synthesize information in novel ways. Creativity can become the medium for complex critical thinking that leads children to make some unique discoveries. Most important for gifted students are the many ways that creative instruction impels them to become active, innovative participants and even contributors to the subjects they are studying.

*Principles for Developing Program Content.* To develop challenging courses for young gifted children, the planning committee should have a clear set of standards to guide the process (e.g., Vydra & Leimbach, 1998, p. 464). These standards emerge from the philosophy and objectives of the program in question. For example, if a program is intended to minister to the creative, experimental, and inventive dimensions of giftedness, the standards used for reviewing proposed courses might focus on the following components:

- Course includes topics that will hold the interest of young children for the duration of the program
- Course has plenty of hands-on activities and offers many creative catalysts to elicit new and innovative responses
- Instruction is more a workshop than a lecture format
- Teacher assumes a mentorship role and provides supportive but much-needed critical feedback to students' ideas and their implementation
- Proposed projects and activities are developmentally appropriate
- Content challenges and stimulates children to use higher level thinking and allows students who are highly gifted in a subject to advance and expand without a ceiling imposed on his or her thought and application
- Students have many opportunities to work closely with other young gifted children in the class
- Activities and projects have a sequential development that builds on student skills and helps to bring about breakthroughs in individual achievement and self-expression

These components can be broached in the first meetings with prospective teachers while discussing their course content and activities or when reviewing the progress of the program at staff meetings.

These priorities are the threads that weave different courses together and ensure a consistency in emphasis, tone, and experience as children move from one set of activities and projects to another. Program directors need to articulate their philosophy, goals, and course offerings to parents and school administrations so that they can make informed choices for children. Gifted programs often have quite different philosophies and content; parents and administrators will work together better if they know what these are. Some families, for example, are seeking an accelerated program in math or science—a demanding academic course of study with an emphasis on mastering specific content. Others want nearly the opposite: a break from the regular classroom (especially in summer) that enables their child to be creative, take new risks without the fear of grades, and enjoy the companionship of other young gifted children.

Once program developers have a clearly articulated set of standards for the curriculum, they can begin to design course content—or at least outline areas of study where teachers can create courses. There is more freedom for developing curriculum in a gifted program than in a school. As independent agents (often supported by universities or institutes), gifted programs can target specific educational gaps that program developers have identified in the regular schools. The pressures on regular classroom teachers often preclude the possibility of meeting the creative and kinesthetic needs of gifted children. But in independent programs, students can engage actively and creatively in the process of learning through hands-on experiments, activities, and projects that challenge and intrigue them. Gifted children need to *do* things. Many of them lack the opportunity to find out what they can do. Hence, it is rewarding to see their own ideas, designs, solutions, and innovations in situations where they can explore multiple options and network with other bright students.

It is important to involve the teachers hired for a program in the development of a curriculum. In my own experience, curriculum design is a collaborative effort between the director and the teachers, rather than an established structure imposed on the faculty. The director provides the parameters and working principles for developing the content, and the teachers explore projects and activities they think will apply to the needs and interests of young gifted learners. Ideas should be refined, focusing primarily on the following questions: What will the children *do* with this? Will the students have the latitude they need to tackle the project from multiple perspectives? What about children who have an unusually sophisticated understanding of this particular field? Do the activities challenge students at different levels of knowledge and giftedness and stimulate new growth and innovation? Content should stimulate cognitive growth and advance both critical and creative thinking, instead of merely providing an enjoyable diversion.

Gifted programs have the unique advantage of including courses students would rarely find in the regular school system. Young gifted children can thus develop a new passion for fields that they would ordinarily never discover until many years later. This is always a thrill for the director of a program to see, and it demonstrates a clear need for a wider range of subject offerings to meet the interests and intellectual hunger of gifted students. Teachers also come alive in an environment where they can use some of their most imaginative ideas in a subject. A synergy often occurs between teachers and young children who keep generating new ideas and creative alternatives to the projects presented in class.

# FOLLOW-UP

Ongoing assessment is always important in a gifted program, as the previous chapter makes clear. This is particularly true for young children who may not articulate their feelings about the projects they are doing in any clear way. In this respect, parents can play a significant role. Young children are often more inclined to share their feelings about the program with parents—on the way home or while walking through the halls to class—and parents can then translate these responses to teachers. Parents are also typically better gauges of their children's feelings than teachers, who only see their children for a limited time. Parents can thus provide a mine of useful information.

During the early stages of a program, there is often a great deal of informal assessment and communication going on. Children talk freely to their parents, parents communicate with the staff or teachers, and teachers talk to the children and parents. The program administration needs to create an open atmosphere where families feel free to express themselves—for example, to request a change if their children want to transfer to another class. In this way, there will be few surprises at the end of the program when a more formal assessment happens. If the program maintains small classes, teachers can monitor each child's progress more closely and establish a classroom culture where each student contributes to the development of course content. Some teachers I know have sent a simple questionnaire home to parents that asks the following: What do your children enjoy doing most in this class? What do they like least? What would they like to change if they could? What would they most like to do if they had the choice to do anything they liked? Teachers often send these questionnaires out halfway through the program as a way of assessing the students' responses to the class. Parents appreciate the fact that a teacher cares enough to get their children's responses *before* the program is over. This provides an important opportunity for teachers to receive feedback in a way that is natural for young children—through their parents.

Staff meetings are also useful venues for ongoing assessment. Time can be allotted at each session for teachers to talk informally about the progress they are seeing in their classes and to share ideas on how they have resolved various difficulties. "Too many cooks spoil the broth," as the old saw goes, and gifted students all tend to be cooks. Frequently, even the youngest gifted students have their own ideas about the direction the class should go, and it takes extraordinary patience, flexibility, and imagination for teachers to negotiate these complexities. In cases where teachers are less familiar with issues facing young gifted, staff meetings can provide a forum for teachers to problem solve and share insights.

At the end of the program, a more formal assessment takes place. The exchange of information between teachers, students, and parents becomes even more critical in the case of young gifted children in special programs. Parents want and expect a qualitative assessment of their children of the sort that is generally lacking in preschool and early grades. They desire information on the activities, assignments, and projects their children do in the laboratory, the workshop, and the art room, and on the stage, as well as an appraisal of their learning styles and interests. On their side, the program administrators want to know specifically how the children benefited from the course offerings and how parents felt about their children's experiences. Even the children sometimes take an interest in the evaluation process, discovering more about how they learn best and how they can take their new interests and learning further.

## CONCLUDING THOUGHTS

Many schools in the United States today do not test children until the end of the second grade, and even then, testing does an inadequate job of identifying many young gifted students. Programs can fill a needed gap when other opportunities for academic and creative stimulation seem scarce. Designed by gifted educators who understand the unique needs of this population, these programs play an important role in exposing young students to ideas and activities that enable their talents to develop.

Programs also provide a unique opportunity for parents who are looking for ways to support the talents of their young gifted children. During class time, program administrators can bring in gifted experts for seminars where parents can get current information on gifted issues and network with each other. In addition, a program's teachers can share insights and connect parents to other sources that support their children's talents.

Gifted programs create a community of caring people who understand the importance of special education for young gifted students. This community can make all the difference for families in need of moral support and practical information on how to provide the education their children need.

# 3

# *Identifying and Selecting Teachers*

*Norman J. Mirman*

Any discussion of qualifications and attributes of teachers of the gifted must necessarily be preceded by an examination of the specific nature and needs of the gifted child and of the benefits and pragmatic payoffs accruing to the larger society. It can justifiably be argued that all children should have teachers who are academically qualified, caring, and supportive. This is a given. What needs to be added is that because of their genetic endowments and traits, gifted children need teachers with specific qualities and sensitivities. The selection of teachers for gifted young people, therefore, is a problem of greater magnitude than the selection of teachers in general.

## LEARNING NEEDS AND CHARACTERISTICS OF GIFTED CHILDREN

Teaching the gifted demands more than just good teaching. Gifted students have five particular needs that require special consideration in establishing the proper classroom climate:

1. Acceptance and support for giftedness

2. Access to personal and material resources for learning

3. Independent opportunities to learn instead of being dominated and regimented

4. Right to unique interests

5. Content that deals with principles, concepts, and understanding, rather than with sequential detail (Martinson, 1962)

Children considered gifted fall within the upper 2% of the population in intelligence. This may be the only characteristic they have in common. How individual and varied they are! One may be bursting with questions—challenging, offbeat, irreverent questions; another is quiet and thoughtful. Many have an enormous range of interests; some are single-minded. We see in some the impatient, imaginative, racing mind; others observe the world around them with a contemplative, still attention. Many are frank in their appraisals; most are quite sensitive in their appreciation of people and things. Their sense of humor may be mature and sophisticated or zany and wiseacre. Many have nearly total recall. A child who seems to be merely fiddling on the edge or paying little attention will later remember the slightest detail of what was shown or discussed. Where the average child is curious, the gifted child is insatiably inquisitive. Indeed, gifted children may seem difficult at times because they take the usual childhood trials and carry them to great extremes. However, this also makes them especially perceptive, exciting, and wonderful to be around. Most of all, the gifted child needs what every person needs—love, encouragement, and pride.

Gifted students have many other characteristics that influence their learning. Among these are keen powers of observation, high performance in abstract and conceptual thinking, and ability to synthesize a vast amount of theory and information; interest in cause-effect relations; appreciation for structure and order; high level of retentiveness; verbal proficiency; intuitiveness and empathy for others; high energy; alertness and eagerness; powers of concentration; independence in work and study; persistent, goal-related behavior; and friendliness and gregariousness (Seagoe, 1959).

## TEACHER QUALIFICATIONS

In view of the foregoing discussion of the unique characteristics of gifted children, how indeed do we identify and select their teachers? It would seem appropriate that we approach this from three standpoints:

1. The teacher's personal qualities

2. The specific nature of the program and activities she or he is administering

3. The various aspects of the classroom environment being provided

It would seem fundamental that the teacher of the gifted should have a positive attitude toward high-ability children. Research studies have indicated that teachers possess certain basic attitudes, causing them to either reject or accept superior intellect. Many teachers, like their counterparts in every walk of life, are staunch defenders of the status quo. Some consider special programs undemocratic or conducive to personal or social maladjustment. Others feel threatened by the child with the brilliant mind and try to suppress it. It is important to recognize that although a program of teacher education may alter these attitudes to some extent, some teachers will never overcome these feelings.

It is important that all teachers of the gifted enjoy being with children. This is true of all teaching, but with gifted children, who can find so many ways to manipulate and/or negotiate, it is particularly important to genuinely enjoy their company. Teachers can then deal with their needs and behavioral habits from a positive position. Being organized, observant, flexible, able to laugh at the appropriate time, and consistent in working with children are important qualities. The teachers of the gifted must be mature and secure enough within themselves to be able to handle bluffs and frauds without feeling threatened. They should recognize the limits of their own knowledge and seek sources cooperatively with the students.

The following question has been asked: Is it really essential that teachers of the gifted have a high level of intellect? Our experience indicates that an exceptional intellect and reasoning ability are necessary. It is widely recognized that brilliant minds flourish in the presence of other brilliant minds. Just as this is an argument in favor of ability grouping, so too does it suggest the importance of high intelligence in teachers of the gifted. Thus, these teachers should enjoy the world of ideas and feel comfortable with higher level thinking, so common among the gifted.

Must teachers of the gifted have many years of classroom experience? This is questionable because in many cases, this may be a liability rather than an asset. Many experienced teachers lack the flexibility so vital to effective work with gifted children. They have difficulty adapting to unique or unusual learning styles, and they may discourage freedom of expression. Teachers need to have a constructive attitude toward the development of each student's personality and talents. They must be willing to accept and provide for the wide variety of individual differences that exists among the gifted. They must not reject the child who has difficulty with certain aspects of a subject.

Teachers of the gifted must be able to handle extreme disparities, both within a given student's range of ability and among students in the class. They must be prepared to offer a variety of opportunities to help each student realize his or her potential. For instance, consider a student with the motor skills of a second grader but the creative thinking and problem-solving skills of a middle school student. This child may compose an extra-ordinary work in thought but literally cannot express it on the printed page, at least not within the usual span of time given for such a task. Teachers need to recognize this problem and offer appropriate alterna-tives, such as longer periods of time to write or permission to type or record the work on tape instead of writing it by hand.

Teachers of the gifted also need to have creative ability to inspire cre-ativity in others. Their own values must support creativity. All too often, teachers discourage rather than encourage creative behavior. It seems more important that pupils do their work on time; be energetic, industri-ous, obedient, and popular among their peers; and be willing to accept the judgment of authorities. Such a set of values, Torrance (1962) suggested, is more likely to produce pupils ripe for brainwashing than ones who can think creatively.

The highly creative child may appear unkempt, unambitious, diver-gent, and, in some cases, even rude. Creative teachers foster an attitude of searching, problem solving, and inquiry among students. They do not insist on one correct answer or one correct sequence of steps to arrive at solutions to a problem. Instead, these teachers encourage the testing of hypotheses and the analysis of mistakes. They promote experimentation within an atmosphere of free inquiry. Their goal is to channel the divergent thinking of bright students and not to dominate or frustrate it.

The teachers of the gifted should work constructively to develop high standards of achievement and encourage excellence among students. This in no way conflicts with a respect for individuality or freedom of expres-sion. Creativity is not stifled by an insistence on reasonable adherence to the rules of spelling and grammar in common usage. The teacher can set a high standard of accuracy with no use for the slipshod or the almost cor-rect and still have a deep sensitivity to the problems and difficulties each child experiences in living up to his or her potential.

Because of heightened sensitivity, intuitiveness, and empathy for others, gifted children need special emotional support and understanding. They also require more social support and peer acceptance than the aver-age child. The teacher needs to show them respect and thereby foster the development of a positive self-concept (Colangelo & Davis, 1997).

A vital quality in all teachers of the gifted is a sense of humor. Bright children are quick to see the humorous aspects of a situation, to play on words, and to enjoy a clever joke or pun. At times, this sense of humor may not endear them to their classmates or teachers, yet this is an opportunity for the teachers to demonstrate their appreciation and affirm these students' abilities.

Teachers of the gifted should have the capacity to think about their own thinking, so that they themselves go on learning. They should be able to share experiences with students without imposing controls and inhibitions and to work out rules and guidelines in the process of building social relationships. Participation and collaboration with the students can provide the groundwork for an ongoing perception of identity. Such teaching requires effort, hard work, and attentiveness (Sellen & Birch, 1980).

In her visionary article on teacher competencies, Dr. Sandra Kaplan (1989) reorganized the previous literature, listing five basic competencies:

1. To develop an appreciation for scholarliness and intellectualism. This provides students with multiple and varied opportunities to experience a scholarly environment.

2. To create an atmosphere wherein gifted students develop an understanding of productivity and a sense of industry. This provides students with opportunities to plan and execute their own work and foster independence.

3. To stimulate awe and wonder. This provides students with opportunities to reexamine the world in order to uncover elements within it that activate a sense of wonder.

4. To develop an awareness of intellectual stamina.

5. To develop intellectual leadership. This enables gifted students to acquire the knowledge and skills they need in order to use their giftedness to influence other people and situations.

As is the case with the characteristics of teachers of the gifted, the nature of preservice training for future teachers of the gifted and talented is indeed varied. Some years ago, a committee of the Council for Exceptional Children developed some general criteria for the preparation of teachers of the gifted. The committee believed that teacher trainees needed the following:

(a) high-level competence in at least one academic area;
(b) opportunities for independent inquiry and research;
(c) the study of some topics in great depth;
(d) specialized work . . . planned individually on the basis of need;
(e) understanding of the meaning of exceptionality . . . in relation to all children;
(f) a commitment to differential education for the gifted;
(g) understanding of learning theory . . . [of] higher conceptualization processes, [of] qualitative difference in levels of thinking and [of] the development of cognitive abilities;
(h) study of various provisions for the gifted;
(i) [understanding of] curricular planning for the gifted;

(j)  observation of and participation with gifted children; and

(k)  student teaching with gifted pupils. (National Society for the Study of Education, 1979, pp. 279-280)

Opinions differ as to whether preservice programs for teachers of the gifted should be at the undergraduate or graduate level. At present, there are relatively few undergraduate programs. It should be noted also that studies of successful teachers of the gifted typically have dealt with their characteristics and behavior more often than with their specific preparation (Marland, 1972).

## APPROPRIATE PROGRAMS AND ACTIVITIES FOR THE TEACHER'S CLASSROOMS

With these teacher qualifications and competencies in mind, what ought to be the specific nature of the programs and activities a teacher should carry on in the classroom? The setting for these programs would be one of total ability grouping, either as a separate school for highly gifted children, such as ours, or a magnet school within a school, similar to those that exist within some large urban districts.

Such a program needs to provide meaningful content, learning opportunities involving higher level thinking, and the acquisition of advanced skills, always remembering that these are means to a greater end—the moral and intellectual growth of the individual. Thus, the program should be more flexible and adaptable than general academic programs, providing a stimulus-rich, student-centered environment that integrates individual with group activities. Questioning, intended to captivate and challenge the gifted child, is another element of an effective program. This implies finding ways to get the students thinking and discussing, rather than relying on the teacher to lecture and dominate the class. The classroom should be an atmosphere of inquiry and discovery, with emphasis on problem solving and reflective and critical thinking, rather than a mere coverage of subject matter. Standards and challenges should require students to stretch themselves to succeed, so long as the degree of stretching is within the students' reach. Tasks that frustrate or overwhelm serve no constructive purpose.

Boredom is anathema to gifted children, so it is important that the teacher work to keep them learning in a meaningful manner. The classroom needs to provide a blend of individualized and group activities, including field trips and lectures that provide contact with experts in various fields. It should enable the students to develop independence and self-reliance in work and study, allowing for freedom of movement and activity. This freedom does not imply the absence of all restraint or a climate where a student is allowed to do whatever his or her emotional impulses dictate. A complete absence of expectations and standards does not provide optimal conditions for students to grow and mature. Genuine freedom comes from acquiring the attitudes, motives, and skills that inform the students' choices. This is what the classroom must provide (Passow, 1982).

There are indeed times when gifted students need a more unstructured classroom. One of our teachers at the Mirman School calls this "seminar time." Children and teachers sit in a circle and discuss a book they have just finished reading, solve a problem, explore an underwater shelter, or help one another with their work. There are no hands raised. The students must respect one another and not cut someone off, and they are to compliment before critiquing.

A student once asked our middle school Spanish teacher if he could present a mathematical formula to the class that might help to clarify a difficult point of grammar. The teacher's initial reaction, being a language teacher and not a mathematician, was to refuse the request. However, she was secure, flexible, and open enough to give up center stage and accept the offer. This teacher has since incorporated that "formula" into her lessons. Gifted students often see things from different perspectives. How refreshing and enlightening this can be if the atmosphere and the teacher nurture these tendencies!

One student asked if he could fulfill the assignment for an autobiographical project by producing it totally on the computer using Hyperstudio. By allowing him the freedom to complete the project in his own way, the teacher enabled the student to combine two of his great loves—writing and computers. Growth could then take place in both areas. Teachers too set in their own ways cannot create an environment where students can express unique ideas, let alone soar to new heights.

Elective classes are another avenue for providing gifted students with exciting choices and opportunities to go into depth in areas of study most meaningful to them. Model rocketry is one such elective we offer. Students design their own rockets; study the physics of inertia, momentum, and acceleration; and experience a multidisciplinary approach as they prepare to assemble their rockets. The highlight comes when they go out to the desert to fire off their rockets.

Another popular elective involves the use of feature films in the study of history. Students learn to compare and contrast various viewpoints and perspectives. The teacher considers it imperative that students develop "literacy" in the medium and acquire standards to evaluate or judge the quality of what they are watching. For "visual learners" in particular, critical and enjoyable viewing can be their key to greater involvement in the study of history.

An elective in advanced computing enables the students to create an entire project through research, scripting, authoring, and storyboarding. Team members are encouraged to apply maximum creativity, sophistication, and skill to produce a high-quality product. Each student will contribute by providing his or her own input and by cooperating with all team members for a successful completion of this project.

What are the qualities of a "gifted environment"? Such an environment provides room to maneuver but with limits on the amount of room; allows self-determination with basic, justifiable rules of behavior in an even-handed, justifiable manner (freedom-responsibility paradigm); provides external motivation while promoting internal self-discipline; is structured but open to the importance of tangents and deconstruction; investigates possibilities but never loses sight of larger forces; is relaxed but not casual; is physically safe but creatively and intellectually "unstable"; and is demanding but forgiving (Brady, 1997).

The organizational environment is an important aspect of the program for gifted children. This environment may include learning centers developed jointly by teachers and students, multilevel class groupings, mentors inside and outside of class, a richness of resources inside the classroom or readily available outside, and internships. Above all, instructors should avoid being "two-by-four" teachers—teaching solely between the two covers of a book and the four walls of a classroom.

## CONCLUDING THOUGHTS

Cultures thrive when they are guided by a vision of what might be. We are all deciding what our future will be like. By this reasoning, society—from the family to the federal government—ought to be aware of the cultural climate it is providing. It should offer the highest standards of thought, education, and morality. No one's intellect should be a prisoner of circumstances, any more than of heredity. Society has a need for excellence. Gifted children have the potential for excellence, and it is our challenge to provide the educational program and environment that will foster their optimum growth.

Paul Ehrlich (1971), in an article "The Lost Genius Debate," commented,

> Let us be specific. Intelligence has both genetic and environmental components. The latter include adequacy of diet, amount of parental attention in early childhood, general home environment, access to educational opportunities, and the existence of an educational system capable of recognizing and stimulating gifted children. Deficiencies in these factors inhibit the realization of genetic potential. In other words, they suppress genius.

Noting that excellent math and science teachers are in short supply in New York City, Nathan Glazer asked, "If they are scarce, is their effectiveness maximized by scattering them to serve all children or by their concentration so that they can serve the high-achieving?" I think there is a good argument to be made that their effectiveness is maximized by concentration. They, like their students, have peers who can talk to, work with, and motivate them. "While recognizing the potential for inequality," Glazer continued, "I would argue that nowhere do we get so much for so little . . . than where we bring together the gifted and competent. They teach each other. They create an institution with an advantageous label" (Kozol, 1991).

Gifted children are the boys and girls who are being overlooked when, in reality, they are like diamonds. They would bring sparkle to the new century if educators recognized their real value and established a place and process for bringing out their beauty and ability.

There is a continuing need for the development of caring, concerned, compassionate, and committed individuals who use their talents for society's benefit, as well as for their own self-fulfillment.

Let us all move forward toward a tomorrow in which the richest resources of our nation—our gifted and talented children—are challenged and perfected. In the process, we will perfect and fulfill ourselves.

# 4

## *Special Programs at the Elementary Level*

### *Content and Methods*

*Mary K. Pleiss*

Ann's head is full of stories, but she is frustrated by her inability to produce written work of the quality she reads in "real" books. She wants more guidance in her writing, but her second-grade teacher devotes little time to creative writing activities. Daniel wants to be an archaeologist—not when he grows up, but right now. Samantha is bored in her fourth-grade math class because she understood fractions before the school year began. She is much more interested in the algebraic equations her father teaches her at home. Pat develops original computer games and wants to design a Web site so that other kids can play along.

All of these elementary students are hungry for opportunities that traditional school programs, and even some gifted programs, do not provide. They are perfect candidates for special programming such as afterschool, Saturday, and summer courses. If these classes meet gifted students' educational needs and expand their talents, they can bridge current gaps in school experiences and lead to new paths for study and exploration.

Special programs offer time for depth and breadth of study in specific subject areas, time that traditional classroom environments, even those geared directly to the needs of gifted students, may not be able to provide. In specialized courses taught by content-area experts, students explore concepts and topics outside the scope of the normal elementary curriculum: archaeology, conversational French, Native American mythology, papermaking, fractals, and the physics of rocketry, to name a few possibilities. Flow experiences, where awareness of self and time is lost in an intense focus on the activity at hand (Csikszentmihalyi, 1990), rarely occur within the scheduling demands of a traditional classroom, but they can unfold in an in-depth course. Experiences in special programs may also become crystallizing moments when students suddenly become aware of the match between their own abilities and passions and the requirements of a particular domain (Warner & Gardner, 1986). These epiphanies lead students to redefine their self-concepts and their future courses of study.

To provide positive experiences, those responsible for the program must give serious consideration to the selection and implementation of effective curricula. This chapter will explore content, methodologies, and assessment strategies for curricula in special programs for gifted elementary students. Recommendations are based on my experience, both as a past director of Purdue University's Super Saturday program and, currently, as a teacher at the Sycamore School in Indianapolis, Indiana. Super Saturday provides semester-long weekend courses for students identified as gifted and talented in a variety of academic and artistic disciplines. Sycamore is a private school for academically gifted students, offering a fully differentiated curriculum in full-time classes from preschool through eighth grade. Teachers at the school are responsible for developing their own curricula to meet their students' special needs, either by adapting existing materials or by creating entirely new units of study. Afterschool and summer classes are offered to supplement Sycamore's regular program and to further develop students' talents. Although standards for curriculum differentiation and implementation are consistent across program settings for gifted and talented students, adaptations must be made to fit the special circumstances of afterschool, Saturday, and summer programs.

## SPECIAL PROGRAM SETTINGS

Special programs for gifted learners are offered to address shortcomings in local schools' offerings for academically talented students. They also allow students to explore courses of study unavailable in the elementary curriculum due to lack of time, materials, or content experts. Programming ranges from 1-day experiences such as those offered at the Carnegie Mellon Weekend Workshops (Piskurich & Lupkowski-Shoplik, 1998) to full-day classes in a 1- or 2-week summer camp. Many programs meet once a week throughout a school semester or year, either for 1 hour, as in the afterschool offerings of many private schools, or a 2- to 4-hour block on Saturdays.

Attendees include students who have a deep interest in particular course offerings and those whose access to gifted and talented programming options in their regular school is limited by any number of factors, including class size. In university settings, special program participants often come from rural districts where smaller populations make full-time services impractical, particularly in specialized subjects such as the fine arts (Clark & Zimmerman, 2001). Homeschooling is gaining popularity as an option for gifted students (Staehle, 2000), and special programs can supplement a home education.

In a university setting, these programs are often staffed by professors and graduate students who are specialists in their fields of study or by preservice teachers who have expertise to offer in a field of interest to gifted students. Community members and full-time teachers may also be instructors. Afterschool and summer programs offered through elementary schools are typically staffed by the schools' teachers and by interested community members. In all cases, it is the responsibility of the program's director to select and train qualified instructors, as well as identify those students who will most benefit from the program.

## SELECTING EFFECTIVE CONTENT

The most important needs and characteristics of gifted students in the elementary grades should shape the course offerings of any special program. Beyond their obvious precocity, gifted students are insatiable questioners, eager to investigate new phenomena. This drive for fresh understanding requires advanced, rigorous content and challenging educational experiences. Gifted elementary students exhibit periods of unusually intense concentration when they deal with subjects that pique their interest, and they need instructors who can create a focused environment and facilitate their explorations. Because they become capable of abstract thought at an early age, many gifted students are natural interdisciplinary thinkers. They enjoy finding connections between subjects and applying knowledge across domains. This characteristic in turn leads to creativity—the ability to forge new ideas and products based on the connections gifted students sense (VanTassel-Baska, 1998b).

All of these traits set the criteria for special programs and their component courses. Courses should both elicit and satisfy students' curiosity, providing them with opportunities to ask questions and learn the skills needed to find answers that, in turn, lead to new questions. Course content and materials should be aimed at least 2 years above students' current ages or grade levels (Feldhusen, 1991), even in enrichment classes. Classes should focus on real-world applications of knowledge and interactions with the tools, techniques, and worldviews of professionals in the various content areas. Opportunities should enable students to do interdisciplinary work and develop and present original products that achieve more than simply review existing information.

These guiding principles can help program directors and teachers select topics and themes for course development. Highly accelerated approaches and unusual enrichment topics have proven to be popular with special programs students, and both are necessary for a well-rounded program (Feldhusen, 1991). Summer and Saturday programs offer an optimal setting for the Type III enrichment described in the Renzulli model (Renzulli & Reis, 1986), as selective identification procedures and the opportunity for investigations of real-world problems are part of the structure of special programs. Even enrichment classes, however, should offer challenging, rigorous academic experiences. Too few gifted students are sufficiently challenged in their everyday education (Thompson, 1996), and special programs must rise to meet their needs.

Course content may be focused on a particular topic or subject area, or it may be more broad based, with activities and information from a variety of disciplines brought to bear on a central theme. Content that is radically beyond what students normally experience in school most often appears in accelerated courses in algebra, geometry, computer programming, and some science courses such as chemistry and physics. Planning for accelerated courses involves careful selection of both teachers and students. Teachers need strong backgrounds in the content area, and students must have certain prerequisite skills and the capacity to work at an accelerated pace. Careful selection of students and thorough pretesting ensure that participants will have worthwhile experiences in accelerated courses.

In many science and humanities courses, topics tend toward enrichment, with advanced readings and problem-solving activities providing above-grade-level experiences. In-depth studies of science topics not generally covered in elementary school, including archaeology, horticulture, ornithology, and architecture, often prove popular with elementary students. Some teachers also offer creative combinations of scientific disciplines; for example, a course on aquatic life and aquarium maintenance might incorporate concepts and processes from both zoology and chemistry.

Historical topics that receive little treatment in most elementary curricula can be used to great effect in special programs. Students might explore South American, Asian, and African history; pre-Columbian North America; the Irish Famine; the immigrant experience in the United States (especially in modern times); or personal history and genealogy. Elementary students respond especially well to simulations and investigations dealing with the daily lives of people in different times and places.

They might become Oregon pioneers, Roman gladiators, or medieval peasants in their quest to understand the past.

Creative writing and genre-specific literature classes are offered within the language arts strands of special programs. These compensate for lack of attention to such areas as student publication, complex poetry, biography, science fiction, and fantasy literature in the basic elementary curriculum. Special programs are in a unique position to offer intense experiences in other language arts, including public speaking and drama. These processes allow students to use their writing and reading in new ways as they learn about oral and visual applications of language skills. Foreign languages, when taught in conjunction with explorations of the originating cultures, provide opportunities to gain a deeper understanding of different people and nations, as well as new insights into the structure and context of our own language (Thompson & Thompson, 1996). Students may incorporate new language skills into videotaped "news broadcasts"; presentations about art, culture, and politics in other countries; and correspondence with foreign students who speak the target languages.

Courses in fine arts allow elementary students to discover and develop new talents. Although students in most elementary schools might be lucky to spend two or three 40-minute periods per year working with pottery, a Saturday or summer class may provide 10 or more hours to explore various media and techniques needed to express oneself in clay. Younger children can learn about the concept of patterns in art by exploring a full range of media, including block prints, paint, tiles, and textiles. Music courses can cover history, theory, and composition as well as performance. In advanced arts courses, entrance criteria may be highly selective, but for most elementary courses, student interest, rather than experience, should be the determining factor in selecting enrollees.

One alternative to single-subject classes is the concept-based, or thematic, course. Thematic courses present students with a variety of experiences and activities centered on an overarching concept. A thematic course on heroism, for example, might involve students in reading mythology from a variety of cultures; researching heroic figures in history, science, and mathematics; conducting debates on heroic qualities; engaging in leadership activities to build confidence in their own heroic characteristics; and creating multimedia presentations about heroes in their communities. The concept of evolution lends itself to a wide range of activities in archaeology, anthropology, genetics, horticulture, and zoology. It relates to studies of the changes in building styles within the local community since the introduction of computer technology; analyses of the evolution of personal styles of artists, writers, and musicians; and the use of statistical analysis and computer spreadsheets to graph evolution within a given content area.

The key to developing strong thematic units is selecting the right concepts. Concepts should be broad and wide-ranging, rather than limited to a specific discipline. A concept is generally a single idea that prompts strands of thoughts in multiple dimensions: truth, justice, courage, conflict, and beauty (VanTassel-Baska, 1998a). Once the concept has been chosen, curriculum planners can use a web format to map examples of the concept in a variety of disciplines and use that map to plan activities for the course (Robinson & Kolloff, 1994). A team of teaching colleagues might make conceptual connections across courses within a program, thus providing opportunities for students to connect with a broader range of classmates while increasing the scope of their learning. More planning may be required to prepare a concept-based curriculum, but a more realistic, satisfying learning experience is the result.

## CURRICULUM DEVELOPMENT

Choosing a subject or theme is an important first step in building a curriculum, but it is only the beginning. The importance of written curricula for special programs classes cannot be overemphasized. At the very least, teachers should develop lists of course objectives, materials, activities, and assessment protocols. Program directors usually review these documents before the courses start and offer guidance to those who are unfamiliar with course planning or elementary pedagogy. Training sessions are important for instructors who are content experts but are unfamiliar with the characteristics of gifted children and appropriate instructional methods. Workshops can also provide opportunities for teachers to share ideas and experiences and plan joint activities among different courses.

Approaches to curriculum development in gifted education are multiple and varied. One of the most straightforward and easily accessible approaches is the integrated curriculum model (VanTassel-Baska, 1993, 1996). This model encourages curriculum developers to keep in mind three important dimensions: advanced, in-depth knowledge of the course content; higher order thinking skills and discipline-specific processes of locating, applying, evaluating, and creating new information; and a focus on real-world applications and issues related to the topic of study. Teachers integrate experiences in all three dimensions throughout their courses. Thus, students benefit from learning the content, skills, and processes associated with the disciplines studied and become creative producers and contributors.

Another approach that is especially well suited to special programs courses is problem-based learning (Coleman, 1995; Gallagher & Stepien, 1996). Early in a course, students are presented with an ill-structured problem and given roles as problem solvers to handle such situations in the real world. They must conduct research into information, processes, and issues that will contribute to solving the problem. For example, in a geology course, students might be asked to determine the cause of a sinkhole that has swallowed part of a new housing development and make recommendations to builders, homeowners, and insurance agents. Problem-based learning is particularly appropriate for gifted students because it asks more questions than it answers and thrusts students into the unclear predicaments of real life. They must deal with multiple perspectives, disciplines, and approaches to develop solutions.

Although the problem-based learning approach can work in any discipline, most of the materials currently available focus on science and, to a lesser extent, language arts. Many of the gateway to educational materials (Great Explorations in Math and Science—GEMs) units from the Lawrence Hall of Science and the science units published by the Center for Gifted Education at the College of William and Mary use the problem-based learning approach. Although not technically problem-based learning, simulations such as those published by Interact involve students in problem solving and research and are easily adapted for use in special programs.

Whatever framework or approach course planners take when developing curricula, they should keep several important principles in mind. Activities should engage students in thoughtful consideration of ideas and issues. This includes allowing time for debriefing and reflection after learning activities. Gifted students should be encouraged to solve problems and learn the research techniques of professionals in different fields of study. They should learn how to frame questions and discover their answers, the very activities that drive any field of study forward. A diagnostic-prescriptive approach, in which pretests assess students' familiarity with course content, allows teachers to determine starting points, set appropriate paces through the material, and individualize instruction. Finally, and perhaps most important, the course plan must incorporate flexibility.

A general rule of thumb is that teachers should have enough activities and materials for at least 50% more time than the course schedule provides. Incoming students may have more advanced knowledge of and experience with the course content than teachers realize. Often, they will be able to move through the material at a much faster rate than initially anticipated. The needs of individual students may dictate adaptations in content and pace that instructors cannot anticipate ahead of time (Johnsen, 2000). Being prepared for these circumstances will make the course run smoother for both students and teachers.

Active participation and variety are important when developing individual lessons. Students who are interested enough in a course to devote Saturday, summer, or afterschool hours to it will be ready to dive into the material immediately. Just as first graders expect to come home reading after the first day of school, special program students want to get their hands on laboratory equipment, learn French phrases, reenact history, and pour words onto paper as soon as their classes begin. Instructors should resist the urge to give a great deal of background knowledge before students become active participants in the course. In special programs, each class typically lasts at least an hour, often longer. Although this allows for extended periods of concentration, a balance should be struck so that children are not sitting at desks for most of a class. Sedentary activities may be interspersed with those that require movement, change of environment, and a range of groupings.

Rather than lecturing to present new material, instructors should allow students to discover new knowledge on their own wherever possible. For example, instead of a lecture, a history teacher can divide the class into small groups and have each develop questions, conduct research using the Internet and the library, and prepare in-class presentations about the lifestyles of Colonial Americans. In a math class, students can determine the formulae for the area and volume of a cube by using base 10 blocks. While exploring scientific concepts, students may perform demonstrations and draw conclusions from the results or design their own experiments to answer questions they have about new concepts and information. The more abstract an idea or concept, the more important it is to use manipulatives and hands-on activities with elementary students. A balance struck between teacher-guided and student-initiated activities is important as well; students' motivation to learn and progress increases when such a balance is achieved (Rea, 2000).

Meeting guest speakers who are content-area experts and taking field trips to see concepts and processes in action stimulate and inspire gifted students. They reinforce and extend new knowledge and demonstrate the importance of the subject matter in everyday life. Content experts may be either local or, if contacted via e-mail or the World Wide Web, located hundreds of miles away. Contact with these experts brings added depth and dimension to students' experiences, especially if they are willing to share their enthusiasm, knowledge, and expertise. An added benefit is positive publicity for the program in the community at large (Stephens & Karnes, 2000).

No amount of knowledge *about* a field can ever substitute for a practitioner's passion *for* the field in attracting students to its content and methods. Field trips into the community are equally beneficial. A drama teacher might take the class to a local theater where they meet actors and directors and learn how to apply makeup, choose effective costumes, and move comfortably on stage. A science teacher might invite a pilot to explain how the laws of physics allow his airplane to fly. Community and university resources can add a valuable dimension to the curriculum at little or no cost. Professionals, experts, and graduate students are often eager to share their passions, and they may even develop into mentors for students with talent.

During their courses of study, students should be engaged in the full range of work done by professionals in the fields they study. To perform, actors study literature, memorize, apply makeup, and collaborate with directors. When scientists experiment, they write and present their results, draw conclusions, and develop new questions for research based on their previous findings. Writers must know how to absorb and use experiences, edit, publish, and sometimes even collaborate. Artists must know about the chemistry of their media, effective display techniques, and gallery openings. Historians interview eyewitnesses, examine photographs and original documents, and draw conclusions from data. Whenever possible, students should have similar experiences. Brainstorming with instructors in other fields and careful planning will illuminate interdisciplinary connections for teachers, so that they can make them real for their students.

Products and presentations are vitally important components of special programs classes. They may be the focus of the whole class, as in a creative writing or drama course, or cumulative reflections gained from independent experiments in a chemistry class or the study of culture in foreign language courses. These should require appropriate research methods and effective presentation techniques, whether the setting is a science fair, a book signing, a poetry tea, or a probability carnival. The aim is true synthesis of creative thinking and applications, rather than just reporting information.

Whatever forms their projects take, students will need plenty of time to develop research questions, conduct investigations, and create appropriate presentations. Practice of presentation techniques, whether it takes place in class or at home, is required to build confidence. The final presentations should have real-world audiences who include one or more content-area experts as well as friends and family. Experts can ask relevant questions and make authentic assessments of projects. Projects should be attractively displayed and promoted; this boosts student self-esteem and reinforces the value of the courses (Stephens & Karnes, 2000).

Homework is another important component of special programs classes, especially those that do not meet on a daily basis. Homework assignments reinforce skills and patterns of thought that are important for learning the discipline in question. The key is to make the assignments interesting and relevant. First graders in a foreign language course might label furniture and household objects with their French names. Third graders working on a problem-based learning unit about an oil spill might conduct library or Internet research on the kinds of animals living in the biome affected by their problem and present their findings at the next class meeting. Fifth graders in a statistics class might survey the music preferences of their peers and graph the results. Applications and extensions of the course content, especially those that involve their daily lives, friends, and families, will make the material real for students and increase interest in the subject matter.

There are nonacademic considerations to keep in mind as well. Because of their learning differences, gifted students are often unique, and therefore isolated, in their daily classroom settings. Special programs provide opportunities for socialization with others who have similar talents, sensitivities, and thinking processes. When planning classes, teachers should allow a healthy amount of time for interaction among classmates, from first-day "ice breaker" activities to small group projects and exchanges of addresses on the final day.

Parents should be provided with information about the course as it progresses. Sharing course syllabi, weekly newsletters, and homework assignments with parents will keep them advised of course expectations and help them to reinforce learning objectives at home. When students present individual and group projects, parents provide convenient and appreciative audiences. Some programs even offer courses to help parents better understand and meet the needs of their gifted children.

# ASSESSMENT

Cumulative and summative evaluations are important for the success of students, teachers, and the program itself. Student assessment should begin with some form of pretest. These may range from informal questionnaires on interests and previous experiences with course content to written tests that reflect the knowledge teachers expect students to have by the completion of the course. The former works best with younger students and with subject matter that does not lend itself to written testing; the latter is more useful with older students who understand that they are not expected to know all the pretest material at the beginning of the course and who enjoy comparing their pretests and posttests to gauge their own learning. Pretesting may also be conducted by examining work samples early in the course. In creative writing and visual arts courses, students may keep portfolios of all their works. Instructors and students can then evaluate beginning, middle, and final examples of student works to assess progress.

In all cases, assessment of student work should be specific and constructive and involve students themselves in the evaluation process. Assessment criteria should be made clear to students before tasks are to be completed, so that evaluative judgments and comments make sense to them. If a scoring rubric is used, students should have a copy when the project is assigned. This will give them direction as they plan their work and allow continuous, internal evaluation as they polish and present assignments. Students need to learn to judge their own work honestly. Therefore, final assessments of major projects should allow for self-evaluation, whether through written forms or verbal debriefing sessions with instructors and peers. Students should also be given the opportunity to evaluate their overall performance in a course. A brief questionnaire, asking students to assess the knowledge and skills they have gained as well as changes in their attitudes about course content, will give them the opportunity to reflect on their own learning.

Gifted children are surprisingly honest in such evaluations; often, their perfectionism leads them to be harder on themselves than necessary. Teacher feedback can correct such unrealistic expectations and point out positive growth points that students may have overlooked, as well as offer suggestions for improvement. Teachers may also use assessment points as opportunities to encourage further study and experiences for students with extraordinary talent in the field of study. A few words of sincere encouragement can have a profound impact on the direction of a young person's life; knowing that an instructor believes in one's talent can be the impetus for independent study and even career choices.

Program directors should make every effort to observe and evaluate teachers as often as possible. Like their students, teachers need opportunities to evaluate their development. Some programs ask teachers, especially those who are new to the program and/or are teaching elementary students, to keep journals in which they note the value of particular class activities and reflect on their growth as instructors. Individual teachers and directors should meet to discuss the direction of the curriculum and the development of the teachers' style. Input from parents and students should be used to assess the impact of the course, the quality of the teachers' interactions with students, and the effectiveness of the course within the context of the program.

When evaluating the effectiveness of a particular curriculum, instructors and program personnel need to examine input from all possible sources, including students, parents, teachers, and program evaluators. A questionnaire about the effectiveness of the overall program can be included with a course evaluation. These determine the value of the course to the overall program, as well as the changes that are required to improve the course in future sessions.

## CONCLUSION

For elementary students with unique talents, special programs can be a haven of learning and a doorway to new subjects and modes of thinking. To open these doors and invite students to step through, those responsible for curriculum development must approach their task with a comprehensive knowledge of appropriate content, instructional strategies, activities, and assessment techniques. Such knowledge leads to enhanced, articulated curricula, which in turn provide confidence that all those involved in special programs are, in fact, serving the special needs of our gifted elementary students.

# 5

# *Designing and Implementing Curriculum for Programs*

## *Elementary and Middle School Levels*

*Cheryll M. Adams*
*Sara Delano Moore*

> *"Gifted and talented" is not something you can take up lightly on free weekends. It's something that's going to affect everything about your life, twenty-four hours a day, 365¼ days a year.*

> —American Association for Gifted Children (1978, p. 141)

Designing and implementing curriculum for special programs aimed at gifted students is not vastly different from designing in-school programs for this population. The gifted population is not a homogeneous one; hence, the curriculum must still be differentiated along several dimensions such as content, process, product, learning environment, affect, interest, readiness, and/or learning profile (for detailed discussions of these issues, see Maker, 1982; Tomlinson, 1995; VanTassel-Baska, 1992). We are also talking about qualitatively different curriculum, not quantitatively different curriculum (i.e., we don't give the brightest students more work to do because they finish faster).

As with in-school programs, if we indicate the program is for gifted students, we must be able to defend our decision. To be defensible as a program for gifted students, the curriculum needs to pass the "Harry Passow Test"—Should all kids be doing this? Could all kids do this? Would all kids want to do this? If the answer to all three is yes, we will have a hard time defending the program "for gifted only."

The dimension that is quite often different between in-school and special programs is *time*. The program's duration may vary from several weeks to a full year, and in general, students meet for a longer block of time than what is available during the school day, usually for several uninterrupted hours. Instructors in these special programs have opportunities to use a variety of individual, small, and whole group activities such as field studies, laboratory work, writing workshops, construction, simulations, and methodological activities.

All of these curricular issues—differentiation, quality versus quantity, defensibility, match with identification, and time—must be considered when designing a successful program and writing the curriculum. Although discussed in detail in other chapters, a discussion of curriculum and program development is not complete without mentioning selection of students, faculty, and resources to show the connections between these issues and the integrity of the program.

## ASSUMPTIONS ABOUT SELECTING STUDENTS, FACULTY, AND RESOURCES

### Selecting Students

Identification of students for the program must match the intent of the programming (e.g., use writing samples to identify students for a creative writing program). Students should have a common interest in the content of the program. Out-of-school programs generally supplement the students' interests and abilities rather than "fix" a weakness.

### Selecting Faculty

Instructors must have an in-depth knowledge of the content and the type of student they are serving, and they must be comfortable working with highly able students. Programs for gifted students are not for the faint of heart! A high energy level helps.

## Resources

A variety of primary sources must be available, as well as opportunities to "discover" information rather than being "told," appropriate technology to enhance the experience, and modifications to accommodate the asynchronous development of mind and motor skills (e.g., the student has wonderful ideas to share but does not yet know how to write).

# HOW DO I PLAN AND IMPLEMENT THE PROGRAM?

## Diagnostic Assessment of Student Ability, Interest, and Knowledge

Assessment must match the goals of the program. This does not, however, mean the assessment must be formal. Data can be gathered through discussion, survey, interview, performance, portfolio, and/or testing. When students are assessed at the beginning of a program, this information can be used in the conduct of the course to select individual projects or create groups of students. The assessment should provide data for the instructor to use in making individual placement decisions for the course. Students should not be asked to repeat information, skills, or material once mastery has been documented. The instructor will need to adjust the pace and/or level of instruction based on the assessment information.

## Flexible Curriculum (Differentiation Within Gifted Group)

Gifted students are not a homogeneous group, and programs for them, whether in or out of school, should reflect this. Abilities may be wide and varied, even within this population. Programming should provide for a range of learning opportunities. Students with similar ability level may not necessarily have the same skill level or interest. For example, of two students who score in the 99th percentile on a standardized math ability test, one may be ready for pre-algebra and the other for Algebra II. Two students who have both had 3 years of violin lessons may not both be ready to play Bach's *Air on a G String*. In addition, opportunities to choose activities based on interests, readiness, and/or learning profile in both individual and group formats are essential.

## Intellectual Rigor

Gifted students should do work that has intellectual value. Intrinsic motivation and pleasure are important and often come with the satisfying experience of being successful with rigorous work. Instructors should encourage students to develop their ideas and products to the greatest possible extent, asking questions to expand thinking at every turn. Intellectual rigor exists in all endeavors, not just the traditional academic fields. It is possible, and to be encouraged, that an artistically talented student of quilting would study color theory and textiles in a rigorous way along with the expected study of piecing and applique techniques.

## Process With Content

Many students who have been identified as gifted have good memorization skills and may know many facts about a particular subject of interest. If we expect gifted students to produce information as well as consume it, they need opportunities (both in and out of school) to learn the process skills that connect the facts that they know and lead to the production of new information. For example, a student may know many facts about natural disasters; he or she may still need to learn the processes of scientific investigation associated with meteorology. When teaching specific process skills such as developing hypotheses or learning a creative problem-solving process, it is equally important that the instructor provide opportunities to practice these processes with rigorous content.

## Appropriate Products

The expectations for products created by gifted students should be consistent with the high level of content and process work expected of them. Students should share their work in suitable professional formats (e.g., a research report written in the style of a scientific journal or a formal showing of artistic creations) and receive appropriate feedback about the work.

## Opportunity for Transfer of Knowledge

Gifted students often become engrossed in a single topic of interest and may find connections to this topic in every situation they encounter. These connections, initiated by the instructor or by the student, can be excellent "teachable moments" for the transfer of knowledge. Gifted students are to be encouraged to explore ideas in new and different ways and to transfer their knowledge, particularly of process skills, to a variety of settings.

## Other Issues

When planning programs for gifted students, one should consider three other major issues: grouping practices, coordination of in-school and out-of-school programs, and opportunities for leadership development. Each will be addressed briefly here.

*Grouping.* Gifted students have many different peer groups. They have chronological age peers, intellectual peers, social peers, and physical development peers, just to name some of the possibilities. Grouping can be homogeneous or heterogeneous by any of these peer groups any time students are gathered together. To consider what form of grouping is appropriate, we must ask, "What purpose does out-of-school programming serve?" Well-designed school programs provide opportunities to interact with intellectual peers. If academic needs are met in this way, out-of-school programs may be intended to provide opportunities for interaction with other peer groups. Heterogeneous grouping by intellect is then appropriate. If an out-of-school program is intended to meet intellectual needs by providing an opportunity to explore a subject of interest at greater depth, then students should be with others of similar talent and interest.

A second question around grouping is that of flexibility. Children grow and change over time, especially in intermediate and middle grades. Grouping arrangements should be flexible so that changes in interest, skill, and maturity can be reflected by changing groups when necessary.

*Coordination With School Programs.* As with grouping, coordinating with the school depends in part on the purpose of the out-of-school program. Programs that provide opportunities the school does not are by their very nature complementary to the school program, and thus coordination is not an issue. When a program provides instruction that the school also provides, however, coordination becomes a crucial issue. Fast-paced summer and academic year mathematics classes are a good example. Many parts of the country now have these programs, modeled after the Study of Mathematically Precocious Youth (SMPY) at Johns Hopkins. Students attend afterschool classes 2 to 3 hours weekly during the academic year and/or for 3 weeks at a residential site in the summer. For a sixth grader completing Algebra I in such a program, having to return to school and retake Algebra I in the fall or continue to take General Math 6 during the school day is a punishment for being good at mathematics. It is the responsibility of both the parents and the program administrators to work with schools in these situations to ensure that the student receives credit and placement for his or her work in programs such as this.

*Opportunities for Leadership.* It is often said that gifted students will be the leaders of tomorrow. Just as the gifted should not be expected to meet their own intellectual needs, nor should they be expected to develop as leaders without any leadership training. Schools have limited opportunities for leadership development, and community involvement (discussed elsewhere in this volume) can provide an excellent forum. Many middle schools are becoming involved in service learning, where community service is tied to learning specific curricular content. Gifted students report that they find such experiences meaningful (Moore & Moore, 1997) and can learn much about themselves and the world from these experiences. Parents, students, and program developers should consider ways in which these opportunities can be provided in out-of-school programs.

## WHAT DOES THE CLASSROOM CLIMATE LOOK LIKE?

### Meaningful Work

When high school gifted students are asked to give examples of meaningful academic work from their school careers, they often describe experiences in which they became better people. Meaningful work is important for every learner; an important characteristic of meaningful work for gifted students is the opportunity to learn about the self as well as learning about content and process. A related attribute of meaningful work is an opportunity to connect with peers and with the larger world. Students appreciate being able to share their work with others and knowing that their work benefits others.

### Opportunity to Think Hard, Work Hard

Learning is important to gifted students, and they often enjoy working hard and thinking hard about subjects that are important to them. Intellectual rigor, active inclusion of process skills, and appropriate products all encourage students to work and think hard.

### Intrinsic Motivation

High-quality programs for gifted students should capture and encourage students' intrinsic motivation to learn about topics that are important to them. Instructors should help students make connections between new ideas and a subject about which the student is already excited. For example, a mathematically talented student's attention might be captured by a study of Escher's work in an art class.

### Creativity

Programs for gifted students should encourage divergent thinking. Out-of-school programs can be ideal opportunities to support students thinking "outside of the box" and taking the risks inherent in creative thinking. Choices in products and processes can support students who are learning to think divergently.

# HOW DO I KNOW IF IT WORKED?

## Assessment

Assessment is a key element in both in-school and out-of-school programs, although assessment is often overlooked in out-of-school programs. It should encompass both formative and summative evaluations. Formative evaluations are typically used while students are practicing a particular skill, concept, key idea, and so forth. Teacher observation, student interviews, practice tests, quick quizzes, and other such measures used to capture the student's progress during the course of a lesson or unit are examples of formative evaluation. Summative evaluations are generally used to determine what the student learned over a longer period of time. Examples of summative assessment include unit and chapter tests, end-of-the-week spelling tests, midterm and final exams, projects, and end-of-course assessments.

*Student Evaluation.* As with diagnostic assessment, student assessment during the program may take many forms, including narrative reports, formal tests, portfolio appraisal, juried performances, self-assessment, and peer assessment. Feedback can then be provided to students and parents in a timely manner to encourage further growth.

*Program Evaluation.* Developers of the program may also wish to gather input from students, parents, counselors, and other program staff about their reaction to the program and/or seek assistance from an outside evaluator to facilitate improving the program. Another chapter in this volume, "Assessment: Impact on Children, Parents, and Teachers" (Chapter 13), deals with this process in more detail.

# DESIGNING PROGRAMS FOR GIFTED STUDENTS

The following pages contain two examples of classes that were used in special programs. Both courses were developed for the Summer Scholars Program offered by the Center for Gifted Studies and Talent Development at Ball State University.

# DESIGNING PROGRAMS FOR GIFTED STUDENTS

How do you plan and implement a program?

    Diagnostic assessment
    Flexible curriculum
    Intellectual rigor
    Process with content
    Appropriate content
    Appropriate products
    Opportunity for transfer of knowledge
    Other issues to consider:
        Grouping
        Coordination with school programs
        Opportunities for leadership

What does the classroom climate look like?
    Meaningful work
    Opportunity to think hard, work hard
    Intrinsic motivation
    Creativity

How do you know if it worked?
    Student evaluation
    Program evaluation

## Can Numbers Talk?

Dr. Sara Moore, University of Kentucky

Numbers tell stories (we often call this "statistics"), and this course is intended to help students learn how to read and write the stories of numbers. Innumeracy (Paulos, 1990) speaks most clearly about the consequences of not understanding the numbers we see in daily life, from the weather forecast to interest rates. The two key references for this course are Paulos's (1996) *A Mathematician Reads the Newspaper* and Huff's (1954) *How to Lie With Statistics.* In each case, students are exposed to the number stories we see in daily life and the ways in which numbers can be manipulated to suit different purposes. The title of Huff's book is particularly appealing to middle grade students. A brief course outline is shared here.

### Data Presentation

Data presentation, often through graphs and charts, is the way numbers tell their stories. This section of the course looks at interpreting and creating such charts. Data sets with very large and very small ranges are particularly useful here.

### Data Description

Data description is the study of central tendency and variability. This part of the course looks at averages that do and do not make sense and other ways of finding the middle of a data set.

### Data Collection

Data collection can greatly affect the quality of data available. This section of the course looks at creating surveys, selecting samples, and exploring the problems of testing. Students often see this part as illuminating the game of school.

### Drawing Conclusions

Once the data have been gathered and summarized, conclusions can be drawn and misdrawn. This portion of the course looks at comparing groups, extrapolating and interpolating from given data, and other ways we try to figure out what numbers mean.

Data sets and exercises are available from many sources. The instructor of this course uses the *Quantitative Literacy Series*, available from Dale Seymour Publications (e.g., Barbella, Kepner, & Schaeffer, 1995; Gnanadesikan, Schaeffer, & Swift, 1987; Landwehr, Swift, & Watkins, 1987; Landwehr & Watkins, 1996; Newman, Obremski, & Schaeffer, 1987), and *From Home Runs to Housing Costs* (Burrill, 1994), data sets from the same publisher.

## Medieval Life

Dr. Martha Craig, Bradley University, Peoria, IL

Purpose: To activate students' own fund of knowledge about the Middle Ages and teach them new information by involving them in a multifaceted medieval simulation.

I created a context for a "time machine" experiment, whereby the students would go back in time to 1268 and try to change English history by attempting to take power over the realm. I explained that Henry III, known in history to have been captured and imprisoned because of his tyrannical ways, was really killed in 1264. History records that his son, Edward I, ruled for him until he died and then became king. My scenario is that Henry's enemies, also bad people, killed him, imprisoned his son, and took over the land. The things that have been attributed to Edward were really perpetrated by these enemies of the realm. (I made much of his attacks on Scotland, identifying myself as a descendent of the Craig clan who fought against the English with William Wallace.)

The students' job is to go back to 1268 and learn to be good rulers, thereby changing history. The time machine is a computer simulation called "Lords of the Realm," which has wonderful sound and graphics that seem to transport the players back to the Middle Ages. It starts with the words, "The King is dead," and gives the date as 1268. Participating in this simulation helps students learn about the economic, social, and political situations of this time by having the players take over and manage territories; keep the peasants fed, happy, and productive; and build castle strongholds. They learn they have to keep armies because the political situation is always volatile, and they learn the difficulties of affording the right kinds of soldiers and arms, in addition to convincing people to become soldiers. They have to know when and how to buy grain and plant and how to protect their relationships with people on all levels of society, both enemy and friend. As side ventures, they can go on Crusades or explore Ireland and Scotland.

After about an hour of the simulation, the students reconvene in the classroom to discuss what they have learned. They share strategies ("You can't build an army with only 90 men!") and discuss their reactions to the learning experiences that befall them ("I couldn't find a merchant, so my peasants were starving, and they wouldn't do a thing I told them to do!").

The room is set up with a table of books on all aspects of medieval life. Other activities are set up in the classroom to involve students in the spirit of the experience, the two most important being a table with small lead figures of knights on horses that they will paint and take home and the materials for designing and building castles. The students are given notebooks in which to keep "in-character" journals, and I read them every morning and write comments to guide them for the next day.

Following is a breakdown of activities:

| | |
|---|---|
| Monday: | Explanation of the time travel experiment and tour facilities in room; time travel game ("Lord of the Realm"), bringing notebooks along for noting important strategies; discussion of experiences in time machine; preliminary planning of individual castles; priming knights for painting. |
| Tuesday: | Tour of medieval room at the Ball State Museum of Art with curator; time travel simulation; discussion; work on figures; refer to books for planning castles. |
| Wednesday: | Time travel—by now students are very advanced and have developed ruling philosophies; discussion; paint figures. |
| Thursday: | Time travel; view and discuss David MacCauley movie, *Castle*; individual castle building; finish painting and seal figures. |
| Friday: | Time travel; finish castles; get in costume for feast; decorate castle on cake with frosting; medieval feast with Rock Cornish game hens, hard bread, apples, stuffing, ale (Sprite), and cake. |

# 6

## *Designing Math Curriculum to Encourage Inductive Thinking by Elementary and Middle School Students*

*Basic Principles to Follow*

*Christopher M. Freeman*

Tᴴhis chapter is intended to be of interest to anyone working to establish or improve the mathematics curriculum for gifted students in elementary or middle school. The principles I advocate, as well as the activities that illustrate them, may be used either in a pullout program for gifted students within a regular school or in a separate summer or weekend program for the gifted. I developed these principles and activities during more than 20 years' teaching of math enrichment classes in the

Center for Gifted's Worlds of Wisdom and Wonder and Project programs in the Chicago area. These programs run for 2 or 3 weeks in summer or for 5 successive Sunday afternoons in winter. I also apply these principles and activities to my regular teaching work at the University of Chicago Laboratory Schools. In our middle school schedule, we have a weekly "Activity Period," during which students may sign up for a variety of enrichment activities, including math. My sixth-grade students may also sign up for the "Long-Term Activity," which requires a 5-week commitment. Both of these activity periods constitute an effective pullout program, in which all our students enjoy pursuing stimulating activities in areas of their own special interests. Several students attend just about every math elective I offer.

In my years as a math teacher, I have become convinced that the math experience for gifted students should include the following:

1. The basic curriculum (for all students)

2. A math team, open to all students, by their choice

3. Enrichment activities, open to all students, by their choice

Although the focus of this chapter is on the enrichment activities, I also have a few remarks on the basic curriculum and the math team.

## THE BASIC CURRICULUM: A FEW REMARKS

First, I need to say that all students must master the basic math curriculum, including the arithmetic of integers, fractions, and decimals; models and applications for addition, subtraction, multiplication, and division; and properties and skills of algebra, geometry, probability, statistics, and so on. Enrichment activities do not replace standard content. It would be a disservice to a gifted student to allow him or her to neglect development of basic skills. Even high intellect needs a foundation of competence. Responsibility for homework is an essential characteristic for a scholar and engenders dependability for use in any activity. The discerning teacher, however, may judge how much practice is appropriate for individual students and require more or less to meet individual needs. Curriculum compacting may be a helpful tool to avoid requiring unnecessary repetition of skills for which a student can demonstrate proficiency.

Second, the basic program must include both abstract and practical mathematics. Students should develop an appreciation for the beauty of fundamental mathematical properties, and they should be able to apply math in a wide variety of uses—from finance to physics, from statistics to art, from business to travel. Many of the problems students are asked to practice on should closely resemble problems that would actually be encountered by an adult in some line of real work.

Third, the basic program must address at least three learning styles: auditory, visual, and kinesthetic. All students need to be able to learn by receiving direct instruction from a teacher. Class discussion by question and answer is valuable for those students who ask, answer, and listen. In addition, all students need to be able to learn by reading written materials, either a textbook or prepared handouts. For many students, the visual is the preferred learning style, and the study of higher mathematics depends on it. In addition to reading, visual representations are essential to mathematics. Graphs of functions are not merely a convenience; for many students, they are the clearest way to perceive and remember essential properties of the functions they represent. I am fond of remarking to my students that, after Descartes developed the coordinate graph, it took only a half century for much of high school calculus to be discovered. Finally, the most neglected learning style in a math class is the kinesthetic. Many students like to work with their hands. Drawing graphs in algebra, drawing reflections or folding patty paper in geometry, measuring accurate pictures to confirm what has been proved in theory, and building models of cubes, cones, or polyhedra provide more than a refreshing change of pace; it is a reaffirmation of self-worth to the kinesthetic students.

## THE MATH TEAM

Students who are gifted in math need to have opportunities to go beyond the basic curriculum. The math team is a form of pullout program that is simple to implement. At my school, math teams meet once per week, during lunch. Math team coaches are paid for extra service, just as athletic coaches are paid.

Gifted math students may participate in several math leagues. The Committee on the American Mathematics Competitions/Mathematical Association of America provides several nationwide contests: the AMC-8 (for eighth-grade students and younger), the AMC-10, and the AMC-12. Top-scoring students are invited to compete at higher levels. Also, many states provide statewide contests, and many metropolitan areas provide regional leagues. Different contests have different formats, which add variety to the activity.

A math team provides the opportunity to work on more difficult problems. True, the problems are artificial, and they are constructed specifically to be hard. But if they are addressed in the spirit of solving puzzles, they can be fun. To make the practices more appealing to students, I took 6 years of previous contests, cut them into separate problems, and reorganized them by topic. Each week for several months, we practice problems from one or two topics. My team members seldom lose interest, and we generally earn among the top scores in the state.

A math team can be a cooperative endeavor. Perhaps only the five top scores will represent the school, but no one can say in advance *which* students will be the top five in any given contest. It is to everyone's benefit that all members of the team improve their scores. A sense of camaraderie can develop, just as on a good athletic team. An excellent team may have a star mathlete, but to be competitive at a high level, the star needs the support of several other students who score nearly as high. Depth is as important in math as it is in basketball. Every member of the team needs the support of all the others. All team members contribute to the overall result.

A math team should be *voluntary.* Although the teacher may invite especially able students to participate, every student should feel that it is his or her free will to belong. There are few opportunities for choice in a student's academic life; student commitment will be far stronger if the student has chosen to devote his or her time to this activity.

A math team should involve a *commitment.* The coach should take attendance each practice session. Only students who attend more than, say, 70% of the practice sessions should be "on the math team" and appear in the math team yearbook photo.

Math contests should be open to all. Sometimes, unexpected students do well on a contest. Their scores may help the school total, and it may be a boost to their self-esteem to know that they are better at math contest problems than they had realized.

Some contests can be required. Our Illinois Council of Teachers of Mathematics offers three individual contests each year; each one is just 8 questions in 20 minutes. I give them to all my sixth graders. If everyone participates in some contests, there is less of a chance for jealousy against those students who wish to take all the contests.

Low contest scores should be kept private. There should be no penalties associated with contests. I always tell my students, "If you do well, you could be one of the top scores which represent our school. If you don't do well, nothing bad will happen, it won't affect your grade, and only you and I will know about it."

## ENRICHMENT ACTIVITIES

The third component of a math program for gifted students is the enrichment activities. These may be scheduled in various ways:

1. They may take class time. For 2 months of school in sixth grade, we play math games for 20 minutes every Monday morning. It's fun to see kids line up at the door, waiting eagerly to get into math class. All students enjoy playing the games; the more gifted students find strategies more quickly and proceed to study more complicated games.

2. They may fill extra class time. I look forward to days when another teacher's field trip takes many students out of my class: It's a perfect day for an enrichment lesson with the remaining students.

3. There may be an elective period available in the schedule. In our middle school, we schedule "Activity Period" each week. Teachers offer activities of interest to them. Students select from a list of 8 to 12 choices, including quiet study and outdoor play. When I offer a math activity for several successive weeks, many students sign up for it at least once, and some students return week after week.

4. For sixth graders at my school, we also offer the "Long-Term Activity Period"; students make a commitment for 5 weeks. Several students attend almost every math enrichment activity I offer.

5. You may provide a separate program specifically for enrichment activities. Most of the activities I use were created especially for the Center for Gifted's Worlds of Wisdom and Wonder and Project programs.

So, what do you do with this time? How do you invent worthwhile enrichment activities? How do you judge whether an activity will be worthwhile?

The activities I like encourage a style of thinking that students don't have much opportunity to practice in either the regular math program or the math team: inductive thinking. In the regular math program, students learn math that has been discovered by others. In the math team, students solve problems that have been created by others. In the enrichment activity, students should have the opportunity to invent math for themselves.

A clear directive to me about the need for inductive thinking came from an offhand remark made by my professor at the University of Chicago, Dr. Zalman Usiskin. He pointed out that, for 12 or even 16 years of mathematics instruction, students are judged by their ability to apprehend mathematics that has already been formulated by others. Then, when they begin work on their PhD, they are expected to discover something new—and they sometimes have no idea how to proceed. When I heard this, I thought to myself, Why not give students the opportunity to formulate mathematical principles while they are young? Over many years, I have developed activities that do just that. I present a situation of some mathematical interest, let the students explore it, and encourage them, through leading questions, to formulate the fundamental mathematical principles that govern it. This process is inductive thinking. I believe it to be of very high importance.

The essential activity of Earth's greatest luminaries has been to discern and formulate the fundamental principles that govern the universe. When the basic principles are understood, everything else finds its natural place in the cosmos. The laws of celestial motion enabled Kepler to explain the motions of the planets. The basic principles, termed *natural law*, were implemented by the Founding Fathers into the Declaration and Constitution. The laws of economics, correctly interpreted, improve the productivity and effectiveness of businesses and nations. The law of non-violence ushered in civil rights. In all fields of human endeavor, not the least in mathematics, the search for fundamental principles is of utmost importance, and finding and applying them brings great progress and joy.

It is a pity, then, that so often the process of discerning general principles is lost in a math curriculum. We tell our students the general theorems, then give them exercises to practice them. We teach the better students how to prove the theorems, but do we allow them to participate in their formulation? Is not the discernment of a theorem a process of importance at least equal to its proof? When I teach high school geometry (often to eighth graders at my school), I provide the opportunity to think inductively: Students spend time in class exploring special cases and inducing that day's theorem before we prove it. (We spend much time in class using *The Geometer's Sketchpad* (Key Curriculum Press), a fabulous tool to encourage inductive thinking.) Ah, but there's the rub: Inductive thinking takes time. In my regular classroom, I find the investment is amply repaid in increased motivation. In my enrichment classes, the time is there waiting to be used.

## BASIC PRINCIPLES FOR INDUCTIVE ENRICHMENT ACTIVITIES

Making worthwhile use of this special time has been my goal for more than 20 years of writing curriculum for and teaching enrichment classes. In this work, I have been led to formulate certain basic principles for my own guidance. My first principle, from which all else follows, is the following:

1. Give students the opportunity to think inductively.

By this I mean that the instructor should present a situation of some interest to the students; they should examine several special cases together, and the students should, with greater or lesser guidance by the instructor, discern and formulate the fundamental principle that governs that situation. This principle should then be tested by applying it to another instance and, if need be, revised until all are agreed on its accuracy and applicability. This process is of fundamental importance in mathematics. It is often left out of typical instruction, but it must find a home in a gifted curriculum.

Other principles follow at once:

2. Avoid compressing content into short time.

The less time that is available, the more the instructor must resort to telling the theorems and relying on the students to learn them. Many students become highly adept at memorizing the results of great mathematicians' studies, but the joy of discovery is lost. The drive to cover content is the enemy of good teaching.

Do not misunderstand me; I am not opposing Renzulli's (1977) technique of curriculum compacting. He intends to eliminate unnecessary review and practice; I agree. But with what do you fill the newfound time? Many programs fill the time with more content; I am advocating filling some of the time with inductive thinking—discovery, if you like.

3.   Allow students time to explore and make their own mathematical discoveries.

Several class management styles work well for inductive thinking activities. Almost always, I begin by presenting an idea to the entire group and then set up a challenge for them to investigate. Sometimes, we investigate as a whole group; students tell me their proposed answers or conjectures. I insist that other students either dispute the proposals or verify them, and I write on the chalkboard only what is agreed on. Alternatively, I allow students to work individually, in pairs or in trios. Then, I allow students to come to me with their discoveries. I respond, either by pointing out an aspect they hadn't considered, by helping them to refine their conjecture, or by approving their work and suggesting a new course of investigation. I prefer to respond in personal conversation, but sometimes I provide guided discovery activity sheets that students turn in for me to look at after class.

4.   Keep the activities open-ended.

Encourage unexpected responses. Follow up on student ideas. Rejoice in new ideas. I enjoy announcing to the class, "It just happened! I've taught this topic to hundreds of students for the past 20 years, and every time I teach it, some student comes up with an idea I've never seen before."

5.   Avoid contrived and artificial problems.

The math team is the place for students to work on problems and puzzles devised by others. In such problems, the student works to figure out what the writer already knows. There is a valid place for such work, but it is distinct from inductive thinking.

6.   Avoid repeating the regular curriculum.

One of the prime reasons for offering additional activities for gifted students is that they are bored with their basic math program. If the enrichment activities focus on topics that will later be a part of the basic program, the students are being set up to be bored later. Enrichment activities should go sideways, exploring areas of math that are related to the regular curriculum, use the language of mathematics the child has attained in the regular curriculum, but are not a required part of that curriculum.

7.   Do not grade.

To be fair, grades should be based on clearly defined objectives, which the student has been given an opportunity to apprehend and practice. In an open-ended activity, even the teacher may not know in advance what the student will discover. If there must be an evaluation, it may describe what the student uncovered and comment on how he or she participated in the process, but it certainly should not try to determine a percentage "right" or "wrong."

One of my most memorable comments to a student, aloud in class and on paper, was this: "You have made more incorrect conjectures than any other student in this class." (Pause, while some students snicker.) "On the other hand, you have also made more *correct* conjectures than has any other student in this class." (Pause, in silence, while students connect these two points.) "Trying, failing, and trying again is part of the process of discovery."

8.   Ensure that topics are mathematically significant.

There are lots of great topics out there, not part of the tested regular curriculum, just waiting to be included in enrichment activities. For the remainder of this chapter, I'll describe some activities I have enjoyed developing together with my students.

## EXAMPLES OF INDUCTIVE ENRICHMENT ACTIVITIES

### Nim: Variations and Strategies

Mathematicians have studied Nim games for thousands of years. I have used them in my regular sixth-grade classroom (20 minutes every Monday morning for 2 months) and as enrichment activities for students in Grades 3 through 6 (10 successive days, 50 minutes each day) or Grades 6 through 10 (10 successive days, 90 minutes each day).

I always start with the "100 Game." Two people play. The first player calls out a number between 1 and 10. Thereafter, each player in turn calls out a larger number but no more than 10 larger than the previous number. Whoever says "100" wins.

I play two demonstration games with volunteer students. I always begin with the innocent question, "Do you want to go first, or do you want me to go first?" As I play, I call out numbers in misleading patterns (with dramatic effect) until I say "89." Students quickly realize that whoever says "89" wins. I then ask them to choose partners and play the game and see if they can find other "winning numbers." The ultimate goal is to be able to beat me. The game is then a cooperative endeavor, with the students working together to find the winning strategy. When a pair of students thinks they are ready to beat me, I require that they beat me twice. In the first game, I may lose, but I discern how much of the strategy they have discovered. In the second game, I use a little more of the strategy than they know. When I win, I haven't revealed the whole strategy, but it is obvious to them that they need to do more research. When a student does figure out the whole strategy and beats me twice, I make a public announcement of the victory to the class. I also keep a chart of victors for my own use; students appreciate the reward of getting marked down as a victor. I then privately share my playing technique (how not to reveal the strategy) with the student. He or she is then at liberty to play any other student, and the strategy will stay secret. (The reader will find the strategy revealed at the end of this chapter.)

The other Nim games I play with paper clips. The basic game has five rules:

1. Two people play.

2. There is one pile.

3. It has 13 objects.

4. At your turn, you may take 1 or 2 objects from the pile.

5. Whoever takes the last one loses.

I introduce the game in the same manner as the "100 Game." Especially important is the innocent-sounding question, "Do you want to go first, or do you want me to go first?" When assisting students in finding the strategy, it is helpful to work backwards. Ask, "What can you do if there is 1 paper clip?" "What do you do if there are 2? 3? 4?" "Do you see a pattern in these answers?"

When a student has figured out the strategy for this game and beaten me twice, I suggest variations. The first variation is to play with 15 objects, then with 20. The ultimate game is to beat me starting with *any* number: I say the number, the student must decide whether to go first and take 1, go first and take 2, or let me go first. I have been known to play this game with students while walking on a field trip. It's fun to see other students' eyes bulge when they hear our conversation: "How many?" "6,489." "I'll take 2." "OK, you win. Another game?"

When many students are ready, I teach another variation to the whole group: At your turn, you may "Take 1, 2, or 3." Again, we play with 13, then later 15, 20, or any number of objects. Quicker students proceed to further variations; all students enjoy working on the game that is appropriate for them.

The next variations are "Take 1, 2, 3, or 4" and then "Take 1, 2, 3, 4, or 5." Students with some knowledge of algebra may enjoy listing the winning numbers for "Take 1, 2, . . ., $k$." When they have done this, I ask them to list the winning numbers for the special case where $k = 10$. They have such delight when the winning numbers of the "100 Game" appear!

Another worthwhile variation on Rule 4 is "Take 2 or 3" (but not 1). This game introduces the possibility of *tying* positions because if there is only 1 left, no one is allowed to take it, so no one loses. Some students will even be able to list winning, tying, and losing positions for the general game, "Take $j$, . . ., $k$."

So far we have varied only Rules 3 and 4. To vary other rules, I teach the two-pile game: There are two piles of 6 and 10. At your turn, you may *take as many as you want from one pile* or *the same number from both piles*. Whoever takes the last one wins. This is actually my favorite game of all. One needs to find and list the winning positions—pairs of numbers that you wish to leave for the other player.

Of course, there is the three-pile game, in which you may *take any number from one pile only*, and whoever takes the last one wins. I often start with 3, 5, and 7 objects in the piles. This is the classic game often referred to as "Nim."

(Strategies for all these games are revealed at the end of this chapter. For more variations and presentation techniques, see my book, *Nim: Variations and Strategies* [Freeman, 2001].)

## An Alternative to Pascal's Triangle

This is one of my favorite 1-day activities I discovered quite by accident. I had planned a lesson about Pascal's triangle with a group of students learning English as a second language (ESL). I needed an activity in which they could participate with limited English skills. I wrote on the chalkboard the following pattern:

$$
\begin{array}{ccccccc}
 & & & 1 & & & \\
 & & 1 & & 1 & & \\
 & & 1 & 2 & 1 & & \\
 & 1 & 3 & & 3 & 1 & \\
1 & 4 & \_ & & 4 & 1 &
\end{array}
$$

I then asked, "What number goes into the blank?" Of course, I expected the "correct" response, "6." But the students answered "4" and "5." Instead of rejecting these answers, I considered them. To continue each triangle, I pointed to a place and asked the students what number belonged there and why. The "4" triangle was fairly straightforward. But the "5" triangle led to animated discussion. Students were delighted to discover a variety of patterns to justify their responses. The patterns were horizontal, diagonal, or even vertical. I leave it to the reader to examine this alternative to Pascal's triangle and discover the patterns on his or her own. (The answer to the "5" triangle is revealed at the end of this chapter.)

## Introduction to the Fourth Dimension

When I was a lad of 10, I attended a math enrichment class taught by a professor from the University of Massachusetts, Ethan Bolker. He gave me the following procedure to generate higher dimensional triangles:

The 0th dimension is just a point:

To change to the 1st dimension, add
a new point and connect the vertices:

To change to the 2nd dimension, add a
new point and connect all the vertices:

To change to the 3rd dimension, add a
new point and connect all the vertices:

To change to the 4th dimension, add a
new point and connect all the vertices:

Next, he challenged me to build a three-dimensional model of a four-dimensional triangle. I went home and pondered and pondered. I looked at what I had in the house. Finally, I decided to build my model of straws connected by strings.

When I teach this activity to students, I usually instruct them how to build such a model, but I'll leave that for the reader. Students in Grades 4 through 8 have enjoyed building these models. I've had students go further and build models of five-, six-, and even seven-dimensional triangles. The activity is unusual in that it links a very theoretical concept (higher dimensions) with a tangible, kinesthetic project.

As a full-class activity, I like to fill in the following table of component parts of higher dimensional triangles. There are many, many patterns for students to discover, argue about, and verify. I make no entries until everyone agrees on their accuracy. (Ultimately, Pascal's triangle appears!)

## Component Parts

A similar table, with more complicated patterns, may be created for higher dimensional *cubes*. (Entries to this chart may be found at the end of this chapter.)

| | | vertices | edges | faces | cells | 4-D | 5-D | 6-D | 7-D | 8-D |
|---|---|---|---|---|---|---|---|---|---|---|
| D | 0-D | | | | | | | | | |
| I | 1-D | | | | | | | | | |
| M | 2-D | | | | | | | | | |
| E | 3-D | | | | | | | | | |
| N | 4-D | | | | | | | | | |
| S | 5-D | | | | | | | | | |
| I | 6-D | | | | | | | | | |
| O | 7-D | | | | | | | | | |
| N | 8-D | | | | | | | | | |

## Fractional Approximation of Irrational Numbers

This enrichment activity is thoroughly enjoyed by high school or older middle school students. The goal is to find a sequence of fractions that get closer and closer to the square root of 2.

To begin the investigation with the whole class, I observe that $1^2 = 1 < 2$, while $2^2 = 4 > 2$; thus, $\sqrt{2}$ must be between 1 and 2. This locates $\sqrt{2}$ between two fractions with denominator 1. Seeking a fraction close to $\sqrt{2}$ with denominator 2, we try $\frac{3}{2}$: $(\frac{3}{2})^2 = \frac{9}{4} > 2$, so $\frac{3}{2}$ is too large but closer to $\sqrt{2}$ than is $\frac{2}{1}$. Seeking a fraction with denominator 3, we try $\frac{4}{3}$: $(\frac{4}{3})^2 = \frac{16}{9} < \frac{18}{9}$, so $\frac{4}{3}$ is too small but closer to $\sqrt{2}$ than is $\frac{1}{1}$.

When we try denominator 4, we find that $\frac{6}{4}$ is as close as we can get but that is no better than $\frac{3}{2}$. But we can get closer with a denominator of 5. Putting all this information into a chart, we create the following:

$$\sqrt{2}$$

too small

$$\frac{1}{1}: \left(\frac{1}{1}\right)^2 = \frac{1}{1} < \frac{2}{1} = 2$$

$$\frac{4}{3}: \left(\frac{4}{3}\right)^2 = \frac{16}{9} < \frac{18}{9} = 2$$

$$\frac{7}{5}: \left(\frac{7}{5}\right)^2 = \frac{49}{25} < \frac{50}{25} = 2$$

too large

$$\frac{2}{1}: \left(\frac{2}{1}\right)^2 = \frac{4}{1} > \frac{2}{1} = 2$$

$$\frac{3}{2}: \left(\frac{3}{2}\right)^2 = \frac{9}{4} > \frac{8}{4} = 2$$

Let the students now consider denominators 6, 7, 8, 9, 10, 11, and 12. Some will improve the approximation; some will not. As students continue the chart, they can find patterns that enable them to predict which denominators will be useful, whether the fractional approximations will be too small or too large, and, eventually, how to generate the sequence of fractions without laborious computations. They can continue the pattern so far as to find fractional approximations to $\sqrt{2}$ that are even closer than the calculator's decimal approximation.

A similar investigation can be done with $\sqrt{3}$.

## Modular Arithmetic

A favorite investigation of mine begins with the simple question, What would happen if 4 = 0? Students will readily admit that then 5 = 1, 6 = 2, 7 = 3, and 8 = 4; but 4 = 0, so 8 = 0. Students will then propose that 12 = 0; indeed, any multiple of 4 would equal 0. Now, mathematicians don't want people to think they are silly saying 4 = 0, so they write a third bar below the equals sign, ≡, read as "is equivalent to." This equivalence relation separates the whole numbers into four separate classes: Every whole number is equivalent to 0, 1, 2, or 3:

$$0 \equiv 4 \equiv 8 \equiv 12 \equiv 16 \equiv 20 \equiv \ldots$$

$$1 \equiv 5 \equiv 9 \equiv 13 \equiv 17 \equiv 21 \equiv \ldots$$

$$2 \equiv 6 \equiv 10 \equiv 14 \equiv 18 \equiv 22 \equiv \ldots$$

$$3 \equiv 7 \equiv 11 \equiv 15 \equiv 19 \equiv 23 \equiv \ldots$$

Students who have studied "Nim: Variations and Strategies" (presented earlier) will recognize these four classes as important in the game "Take 1, 2, or 3": When there are $n$ objects in the pile, if $n \equiv 1$, you should let the other player go first; if $n \equiv 2$, you should take 1; if $n \equiv 3$, you should take 2; and if $n \equiv 0$, you should take 3. But these classes have other applications. In years ≡ 0, we elect presidents, enjoy the Summer Olympics, and (usually) have a leap day; in years ≡ 2, we enjoy the Winter Olympics. On the south side of Chicago, east-west streets with numbers ≡ 3 are the major thoroughfares, such as 47th, 51st, 55th, and 59th, near the University of Chicago.

The system that establishes the equivalence 4 ≡ 0 is called "modulo 4" or "mod 4" for short. Students enjoy creating addition and multiplication tables modulo 4. Many interesting patterns appear, including "2 + 2 ≡ 0." (Students enjoy telling their parents that their math teacher taught them this!)

| + mod 4 | 0 | 1 | 2 | 3 |
|---------|---|---|---|---|
| 0 | | | | |
| 1 | | | | |
| 2 | | | | |
| 3 | | | | |

| X mod 4 | 0 | 1 | 2 | 3 |
|---------|---|---|---|---|
| 0 | | | | |
| 1 | | | | |
| 2 | | | | |
| 3 | | | | |

You may ask, Are there fractions in modulo 4? Because $\frac{a}{b} = a\frac{1}{b}$, and we already know how to multiply in mod 4, it is enough to ask the following: Are there unit fractions, that is, reciprocals? Observe that $\frac{1}{3}$ is the solution to the equation $3n = 1$; now recall from the mod 4 multiplication table that $(3)(3) \equiv 1$. These two facts together imply that $\frac{1}{3} \equiv 3$. Students will readily convince themselves that $1 \equiv \frac{1}{5} \equiv \frac{1}{9} \equiv \dots$ and $3 \equiv \frac{1}{3} \equiv \frac{1}{7} \equiv \frac{1}{11} \equiv \dots$. However, any fraction with an *even* denominator doesn't exist in modulo 4. Do decimals exist in modulo 4? No, for "decimals" are really just "decimal fractions"—fractions with denominators that are powers of 10—hence even, hence nonexistent!

Going further, students will enjoy creating addition and multiplication tables for modulo 1, mod 2, mod 3, mod 5, mod 6, and mod 7. The tables are replete with properties for students to formulate. Mod 1 has the unique property that $1 \equiv 0$; indeed, all numbers $\equiv 0$. It is the only system in which $\frac{1}{0}$ actually exists because $(\frac{1}{0})(0) = 0 \equiv 1$. (I'm reminded that one of the basic postulates of the real number system is that 1 does not equal 0; in other words, this postulate cannot be proved.)

Here are some other questions worth asking about multiplication modulo $n$:

1. In any multiplication table mod $n$, observe that the row for $n$ is backwards of the row for $(n - 1)$. Are other pairs of rows related to each other?

2. For a given value of $n$, which numbers have reciprocals?

3. For which values of $n$ can you find numbers $a$ and $b$ such that $ab = 0$ but neither $a$ nor $b$ is equal to 0?

4. For any value of $n$, what is the reciprocal of $(n - 1)$?

5. For which values of $n$ does every number have a reciprocal?

6. In mod 2 and mod 3, every number (except 0) is its own reciprocal. In which other modular systems is every number (that has a reciprocal) its own reciprocal?

7. Can you find value for $n$ in which there are more than four numbers that are their own reciprocals?

# SUMMARY

Mathematically gifted students need to learn the basic curriculum. In addition, they should have the opportunity to participate in a math team and in appropriate enrichment activities. Especially worthwhile enrichment activities involve inductive thinking; they give students the opportunity to discover and formulate mathematical principles for themselves. Students eagerly respond to inductive thinking activities, and they are participating in a fundamental human endeavor—to discern the fundamental principles that govern the universe.

# ANSWERS TO PROBLEMS

### Nim: Variations and Strategies

Winning strategies:

"100 game": Go first and say the following "winning numbers": 1, 12, 23, 34, 45, 56, 67, 78, 89, and 100. They are of the form $11w + 1$.

"Take 1 or 2": Be sure to leave your opponent in these "winning numbers": 1, 4, 7, 10, 13, 16, 19, . . . They are of the form $3w + 1$.

"Take 1, 2, or 3": Be sure to leave your opponent in these "winning numbers": 1, 5, 9, 13, 17, 21, . . . They are of the form $4w + 1$.

"Take 1, 2, . . ., $k$": Winning numbers are of the form $(k + 1)w + 1$.

"Two-Pile Game": Winning positions include {0,0}, {1,2}, {3,5}, and {4,7}.

For further variations and strategies, see my book, *Nim: Variations and Strategies* (Freeman, 2001).

### Alternative to Pascal's Triangle

$$1$$
$$1\ 1$$
$$1\ 2\ 1$$
$$1\ 3\ 3\ 1$$
$$1\ 4\ 5\ 4\ 1$$
$$1\ 5\ 7\ 7\ 5\ 1$$
$$1\ 6\ 9\ 10\ 9\ 6\ 1$$
$$1\ 7\ 11\ 13\ 13\ 11\ 7\ 1$$

A delightful feature of this pattern is that the diagonals (after the 1s and the 1,2,3,4 . . .) are the winning positions of the Nim games "Take 1"; "Take 1 or 2"; "Take 1, 2, or 3"; and so on.

| | | vertices | edges | faces | cells | 4-D | 5-D | 6-D | 7-D | 8-D |
|---|---|---|---|---|---|---|---|---|---|---|
| | | | | Component Parts | | | | | | |
| D | 0-D | 1 | 0 | 0 | 0 | 0 | 0 | 0 | 0 | 0 |
| I | 1-D | 2 | 1 | 0 | 0 | 0 | 0 | 0 | 0 | 0 |
| M | 2-D | 3 | 3 | 1 | 0 | 0 | 0 | 0 | 0 | 0 |
| E | 3-D | 4 | 6 | 4 | 1 | 0 | 0 | 0 | 0 | 0 |
| N | 4-D | 5 | 10 | 10 | 5 | 1 | 0 | 0 | 0 | 0 |
| S | 5-D | 6 | 15 | 20 | 15 | 6 | 1 | 0 | 0 | 0 |
| I | 6-D | 7 | 21 | 35 | 35 | 21 | 7 | 1 | 0 | 0 |
| O | 7-D | 8 | 28 | 56 | 70 | 56 | 28 | 8 | 1 | 0 |
| N | 8-D | 9 | 36 | 84 | 126 | 126 | 84 | 36 | 9 | 1 |

### Four-Dimensional Triangles

In the table of component parts of higher dimensional triangles, each entry is the sum of the entry above it and the entry above and to the left.

### Fractional Approximations of $\sqrt{2}$

$$\frac{1}{1}, \frac{2}{1}, \frac{3}{2}, \frac{4}{3}, \frac{7}{5}, \frac{10}{7}, \frac{17}{12}, \frac{24}{17}, \frac{41}{29}, \frac{58}{41}, \frac{98}{70}, \cdots$$

### Modular Arithmetic

1. Row $k$ is backwards of row $(n - k)$.

2. Numbers with reciprocals are relatively prime to $n$.

3. Any number $a$ that shares a common factor with $n$ will also have a number $b$ such that $ab = 0$.

| + mod 4 | 0 | 1 | 2 | 3 |
|---|---|---|---|---|
| 0 | 0 | 1 | 2 | 3 |
| 1 | 1 | 2 | 3 | 0 |
| 2 | 2 | 3 | 0 | 1 |
| 3 | 3 | 0 | 1 | 2 |

| X mod 4 | 0 | 1 | 2 | 3 |
|---|---|---|---|---|
| 0 | 0 | 0 | 0 | 0 |
| 1 | 0 | 1 | 2 | 3 |
| 2 | 0 | 2 | 0 | 2 |
| 3 | 0 | 3 | 2 | 1 |

4. $(n - 1)$ is always its own reciprocal.

5. Whenever $n$ is prime, every number (except 0) will have a reciprocal.

6. Every number is its own reciprocal in modulos 2, 3, 4, 6, 8, 12, and others.

7. Mod 24 has eight numbers, which are their own reciprocals: 1, 5, 7, 11, 13, 17, 19, 23.

Enjoy exploring math!

# Reflections on Special Programming for the Gifted Disadvantaged Students

*Eileen Kelble*

*And how much youth lay uselessly buried behind these walls, what mighty powers were wasted here in vain? After all, one must tell the whole truth. These men were exceptional men. Perhaps they were the most gifted. Their mighty energies were vainly wasted, wasted abnormally, unjustly, hopelessly. And who was to blame, whose fault was it?*

—Fyodor Dostoyevsky, *The House of the Dead*

America cannot afford to waste the talents of any of its young people. It is the lofty goal of this nation that "all children will learn." But as our population becomes more diverse, and diversity expresses itself in many ways, we need to provide learning experiences that accommodate these differences. This chapter addresses the findings of some of the programs with which I am familiar—programs that have helped gifted disadvantaged students who are not learning at the level of their ability. (Renzulli, Reid, and Gubbins, 1992) "Although the scope of this problem in terms of actual numbers is unknown, educators have become increasingly concerned about the plight of underachieving gifted students across the nation."

The underrepresentation of disadvantaged children and adolescents in programs for gifted students continues to be a troubling problem faced by teachers, administrators, and researchers in the field of gifted education. Numerous educators have addressed their longstanding concerns about this problem and its ramifications. But their efforts to bring change have been stymied by the various movements to restructure American education. For example, immersion may have helped some children, but it has been devastating to the gifted. In addition, our various interpretations of the term *gifted* and the ways we try to identify them have not helped the cause. I would agree that all children have certain gifts, but I maintain very strongly that some have more than others.

Unfortunately, our education system has a deficit orientation to children from other cultures, especially those from low-income families. It is assumed, for example, that poor children who lack verbal skills and do not test well cannot be gifted. Many educators today still do not realize that disadvantaged students rarely show their strengths and abilities on standardized testing instruments. Lacking the experience and exposure to course content that mainstream students bring to a testing situation, young people from the inner city cannot hope for a level playing field with their counterparts from the suburbs. As far as verbal skills are concerned, they often have their own language or dialect that takes precedence over Standard English.

Identification and appropriate intervention for disadvantaged gifted students are keys to a successful program. The importance of early identification applies to all populations but is most critical for the disadvantaged who face environmental conditions in their early years that can hinder the growth and development of their talents. For a long time, educators assumed that programs serving largely middle-class populations could also meet the unique needs of disadvantaged gifted children. However, research and field testing have shown that it takes a more tailored and individualized program to identify and educate the "invisible" gifted. A comprehensive service model can best design and develop programming based on areas where learners have the most pressing needs: academics, talents, creativity, and the social and affective areas. The big question is, Do we address an area of need or an area where the learners have a gift?

Viewing them as a group, disadvantaged gifted children have many strengths and talents that have evolved in response to cultural, socioeconomic, and other factors. Torrance (1998) referred to them as "creative positives," and they range over a broad spectrum of abilities—from problem-solving and cognitive abilities to improvisational and creative strengths. But a number of these children also have severe deficiencies and challenges that many educators find overwhelming. Frequently, a well-meaning person who is trying to help the disadvantaged gifted student will say, "It is just not worth it."

This means that we have given up, probably on the very students who most need our help. Disadvantaged gifted students often turn away from school and mainstream society and use their talents for negative and potentially destructive purposes. With no early intervention, they become vulnerable to the forces that dominate in their neighborhoods and families and among their friends. Hungry for some outlet for their high ability, imagination, and energy, the gifted often find themselves becoming leaders of social groups who create a culture of destructive behavior (e.g., gangs). By the time educators address children in this situation, they find it difficult to believe that there is anything worth saving.

Many educators would like to do something about discovering and nurturing the abilities of these deprived gifted students because they know the potential that exists for change and growth. Stories about gifted underprivileged children who have become major contributors to the world abound. But few hear about young gifted persons who succumb to the depravation and hardship that thwart their efforts to succeed. Nor does the field of education have an accurate estimate of how many gifted young people strive to get themselves out of depravation by using their gifts and talents against society.

According to recent statistics, there are more than 1 million men and women in prison throughout the United States, and every year, 10 million people are arrested and almost as many are released. The juvenile statistics are equally grim. Almost 1.5 million people younger than age 18 are arrested, 600,000 of whom are arrested for crimes that would have been criminal offenses had they been adults.

Many prisons now have schools that are taught by the inmates. They serve three kinds of students: those who want to earn a high school diploma, those who are taking college courses, and those who are struggling to attain literacy. Some of the inmates are self-taught. They educate themselves and then educate others. Some of them even reach the point of being able to teach college courses. Law courses have become popular. The book, *Lifers: Learn the Truth at the Expense of Our Sorrow,* by Richard Wormser (1991), tells the story of the East Jersey State Prison at Rahway, New Jersey, its lifers' group, and its "Scared Straight Project." Anyone interested in working with deprived gifted students should read this book. It provides many clues about talented people who do not make it in our society and desperately need a support structure for realizing their potential.

Today, educators are focusing on how they can reach all children, how children learn best, and how they retain what they have learned. Most of us recall that class from which we remember little, if anything, except maybe the bird sitting on the window sill, the color of the teacher's clothes, or how long it took for the hands of the clock to move from one number to another. When students are asked when they learn best, the answer is always, "When I am interested." So we try to apply what we teach to the real world, assuming that it will interest them. But whose world should that be? Ours or that of the students? We tend to forget that we need to apply curriculum content to the *students'* world, not ours. Therefore, finding out what their world is like is important.

Recently, both state and federal legislation have begun to address the needs of disadvantaged students with money earmarked for special programs. These kinds of programs are not new. Many years ago, a wonderful book, *36 Children,* by Herbert Kohl (1967), became a big seller among educators. The message in this book is a simple but powerful one—that we as educators can and must unlock the potential of the children in our lives. Among these children are gifted youngsters who have so neatly masked their talents that it would be difficult to identify or assess their potential and growth through conventional means.

Several federally funded programs have provided a major impetus for responding to this challenge. The Jacob K. Javits Gifted and Talented Students Education Program has focused specifically on the plight of underprivileged gifted students. The various programs funded by this money have made some large inroads into the problem. In many parts of the United States, dedicated researchers are trying a variety of approaches in efforts to find viable solutions for disadvantaged gifted students. Outstanding examples include the University of Tulsa's SAIL program, under the guidance of Dr. Patricia Hollingsworth (see Chapter 8); the program on early identification of potentially gifted students in Newark, New Jersey (Feiring, Louis, Ukeje, Lewis, & Leong, 1997); and Project Step Up (Systematic Training of Educational Programs for Underserved Pupils) (Sisk & Torrance, 2000).

Another federal project recently funded through the Department of Education is GEAR UP (Gaining Early Awareness and Readiness for Undergraduate Programs). Although it does not specifically target gifted children, it has great potential for locating gifted students from low-income families. We know that in the 21st century, college will be more essential than ever before. Yet, studies consistently show that students from low-income families and their parents do not have the information they need to encourage and guide them to make post–high school education a real option.

GEAR UP promotes access to education and educational excellence through partnership efforts. Starting at the sixth- and seventh-grade level and continuing through high school, it provides information to students and parents about post–high school options and financial aid. Tutors and mentors, field trips, and special activities provide necessary exposure to a range of post–high school possibilities. When disadvantaged students aspire for a progressive future, they become more committed to academics as a link to college or some form of higher education. Through this program, states provide scholarships to eligible students on graduation.

Programs planned for the GEAR UP students introduce them to all aspects of college life, from extracurricular activities to academic work. GEAR UP has particular relevance to disadvantaged gifted students because it provides an ideal vehicle for discovering and developing their abilities.

Out of these and other programs have come many ideas and suggestions for nurturing the growth of gifted disadvantaged students. Certainly, the move toward individualization and the integration of subject areas has proved effective. The National Science Foundation and National Science Teachers Association have made great strides in encouraging more hands-on activities. But they still need to go further in retraining teachers for the classroom and the program's implementation. Some of these "new" programs may sound strangely familiar to educators of gifted children. In fact, some educators have raised the serious question as to what teachers of the gifted should do to differentiate their programs if the schools adopt their methodology for all students.

A key to success with disadvantaged gifted populations rests on the caring qualities educators bring to the classroom. How do we exhibit caring? First of all, it has to be sincere. These students are not the kind who will accept or even trust graciousness. Sometimes, what they most need is someone to sit with them during the lunch hour and talk with them about their interests, listening to the stories about their lives. But caring is not being friends, as many young teachers have discovered. It is more. The three words that were used in counseling for many years—*caring, empathy,* and *understanding*—apply well to the disadvantaged gifted as long as teachers express them with sincerity and judgment (i.e., without appearing like a "pushover" to the children). The students need to identify with the educator in some way and then discover that someone really cares. Only then is it possible to find out what the students' interests really are, and only then can a curriculum be developed to meet their needs, develop their interests, and enable them to learn in a lasting, meaningful way.

At the same time, there are skills and knowledge that disadvantaged gifted students need to learn if for no other reason than to pass a required test. It is then up to the teacher, mentor, or tutor to take the curriculum and tailor it to the students' interests, perspectives, and abilities. One of the biggest problems faced by disadvantaged gifted children is that the curriculum usually does not challenge them. How many times do they have to repeat tasks so simple that they stop paying attention? Gifted disadvantaged students need to learn skills in the context of more challenging and stimulating assignments. Any design to educate these children must respond to their particular learning needs, which means developing a plan for addressing both weak areas (e.g., poor skills, gaps in knowledge, etc.) and exceptional abilities.

Positive reinforcement should be part of the plan and should include the students and their parents, the community, the media, and all schools that the students attend from preschool through high school. Another necessary component is conflict resolution that specifically teaches nonviolent means to resolve disputes, disagreements, and injustices. Gifted disadvantaged young people need to understand and become tolerant of diverse points of view, cultures, and biases and learn how they can take a leadership role in finding solutions to conflicts.

Mentorships have proven highly effective in the growth and development of disadvantaged gifted students. Many have become far more confident about testing and exploring their own ideas. All too frequently, the message we give these students is that there is only one way to do things. This is not mentoring. The learning situation needs to be kept open without the mentors' views dominating. Sometimes, study circles work well in opening up a subject for all to investigate. The group sets the rules and everyone can voice their opinions in an informal, relaxed atmosphere—without confrontation.

Community and school partnerships can also create positive change for local gifted students, for example, in establishing tutoring before and after school. Well-trained tutors can save students from slipping through the cracks of the system. So can policies of prevention that use neighborhood programs and include police, parents, churches, business, and civic and community organizations. Ethical and cultural awareness programs that emphasize common ground on basic values such as respect, responsibility, and restraint bring different populations of a community together for the benefit of the students. Trying to help a student without considering cultural values can sometimes lead to unexpected results, as the story below illustrates:

> Little Salvador had no shoes. The weather began to get cold, yet he still came to school barefooted. His teachers were concerned so they collected money and sent it home with Salvador so his mother could buy him some shoes. The next day he came to school with a present for each teacher but no shoes. His culture would not permit the acceptance of the gift without a gift in return so the family could maintain its respect.

This example demonstrates the importance of cultural sensitivity and understanding in any partnership between the school and community.

Disadvantaged gifted children can also reach their potential through youth opportunity programs and peer counseling. Episodes described by adult teachers reveal that some disadvantaged gifted children have quite sophisticated teaching skills and strategies. When providing feedback, tutors should

- begin with praise and honest appreciation;
- call attention to the mistakes indirectly;
- talk about their own mistakes;
- ask questions instead of giving direct orders;
- let the learner save face;

- praise every improvement, even the slightest; and
- start with the positive before you get to the negative.

Gifted children in general and disadvantaged gifted students in particular tend to disparage their work or at least to feel uncertain about it. When offering feedback, therefore, teachers, tutors, or mentors need to provide specific praise for those aspects of their work that express higher level thinking, imagination, sensitivity, and so on. This way, the children will know that the person has really listened or observed and genuinely cares. After affirming the value of the students' thinking, ideas, artistry, and so forth, mentors can then challenge them to go further by showing them where they can make improvements or extend even more.

It should be noted that one of the characteristics of a creative personality is a high degree of sensitivity. Like most high-ability children and young people, disadvantaged gifted students tend to be divergent thinkers and frequently wonder why they are so different. It is not unusual for creative thinkers to be disturbed and overly sensitive about their own thoughts. They need the support and understanding of adults who can assure them that their divergence from the norm does not make them "freaks." Their hunger for acceptance, especially from peers, may cause disadvantaged gifted students to suppress their most creative abilities to avoid loneliness and estrangement. The pressure from peer groups tends to pull these students away from school. The teacher, mentor, or counselor, therefore, has to tread a tightrope to encourage them forward without making them feel cut off from their peers.

Perhaps the greatest fear many of these promising children feel is the possibility of being ridiculed, criticized, or misunderstood. The potential loss of respect and acceptance by their peers is reason enough for them to mask their thoughts, talents, and gifts. For this reason, teachers succeed most with disadvantaged gifted students when they identify their hidden strengths and find ways to support them without attracting too much attention. Students who become convinced that their teacher really cares and that they possess talents worth saving begin to emerge, step by step, out of the downward spiral that keeps so many from achieving anything. As the following example shows, enabling children to discover their own gifts—whatever they may be—is the key to turning their lives around.

James made it to seventh grade but failed to make it to Grade 8. When his teacher walked into the room, it was immediately obvious that he was an unhappy camper. Fortunately, the teacher recognized James's unhappiness and knew that something had to be done. His whole demeanor was one of disgust. He did not want to be where he was, but he did not know how to get out of it. The teacher began to reach out to solve the problem. As a result of her astuteness, she also determined that he could be a key to her success as a teacher that year.

After a series of unsuccessful attempts she discovered that James was particularly interested in baseball. Fortunately, so was she. She had a fairly good knowledge of the game and so began to teach using baseball and its many facets as examples in her classes. After several weeks, James began to realize that Mrs. Jenkins really did know something about baseball and requested to stay after school to help clean the room and set up for the next day. This was unusual for James as he was always the first one out of the room, almost as though he had to escape. While they were cleaning the room for the day, James asked, "Who is your favorite baseball player?"

When Mrs. Jenkins responded, he frowned and disagreed. A good-natured but prolonged discussion ensued about who was the best baseball player, and soon they began to enjoy the debate.

From some of the other students, Mrs. Jenkins found that James was a child of the streets with no one to really care for him except a drunken father who would beat him and a mother who was never home. James was good at all sports, but his parents had never seen him play. Mrs. Jenkins invited herself to a baseball game; he tried not to pay attention to her being there, but she knew that he was pleased. He became excited over his sports ability, shared his successes and failures with her, and began to ask for her opinion on how he could improve.

Then the teacher had the thought of writing "his" favorite baseball player and telling him the story of James. She asked if it were possible for him to send a picture of himself, autographed "to James." Well, the unexpected happened. The baseball player called and asked if he could take James to lunch some day. James immediately knew when he got the invitation how it all came about. He knew someone cared about him. When he came back from his luncheon with his idol, he was a different young man. The turnaround that he made as a result of this intervention paid off. He was anxious to study and even asked if he could come down to Mrs. Jenkins's house to do his studying because he was locked out of his house from seven in the morning until nine at night, and the climate there was not conducive to studying.

He turned into an 'A" student and got upset with himself if he missed one question on a test. James grew from a failing student to an honor student and is now vice president of a major corporation. His best friends, who did not have the advantage of a caring teacher, are now in a federal pen for life.

This is a true story, and it demonstrates the importance of caring. Interestingly enough, not only did James do a turnaround, but the rest of the students also became more teachable. James had informed them that they had better respect Mrs. Jenkins or he would take care of them. It turned out that he was not only extremely bright but a leader as well.

As educators, we need to look for gifted learners like James. We need to keep an open mind and heart so that we don't miss an opportunity to help the children who may otherwise be forgotten. The color of the skin and language should never be a factor in assessing the potential of a student. This applies especially to any educational situation where disadvantaged gifted students may mask their abilities and talents.

The lock-step approach to education cannot respond to the special needs of underserved gifted children. We need to take a long serious look at who the invisible gifted might be in our classroom, what their strengths and interests are, and how we can help them develop their hidden abilities. If we cannot accomplish this in the regular classroom, we must turn to special programs. It is in programs for disadvantaged gifted students that educators and researchers can create new approaches to the curriculum, explore ways to inspire and stimulate exceptional work, and provide the emotional support that enables the children to take risks. Special programs for these students—be they summer, weekend, or afterschool—can save lives; in many cases, they are the only factor in these children's lives that provides any hope for a future.

# 8

# *University School's Community Talent Development Program*

*Patricia L. Hollingsworth*

"Can one pyramid be this big?" asked one second-grade girl of another. "Miss Parent said it can hold 10 football fields, let's keep moving." It was June and the Oklahoma sky was bright blue. The students were measuring the length of one side of the Great Pyramid. When they finished, they returned to a large sandy area to build their own pyramids in the warm sun. These economically disadvantaged students and their teachers were participating in a summer program of active interdisciplinary learning. This is a summer program at the University School at the University of Tulsa, sponsored by a U.S. Department of Education Javits grant.

University School is a full-school program for gifted children from age 3 through eighth grade. Part of the mission of the University School is to provide leadership and service in gifted education to the community. The workshops focus on active interdisciplinary learning as a way for students to develop gifts and talents. By using active interdisciplinary learning, teachers can help students understand sophisticated and advanced concepts.

## SUMMER WORKSHOPS FOR
## TEACHERS, PARENTS, AND STUDENTS

These workshops are part of Project SAIL, a 3-year U.S. Department of Education Javits grant whose purpose is to identify and develop gifts and talents in economically disadvantaged students. To reach that goal, the program provides in-depth staff development for teachers and promotes involvement of parents in their children's schools. Project SAIL focuses on active interdisciplinary learning as a way to develop and nurture students' gifts and talents.

The Schools for Active Interdisciplinary Learning (SAIL) project is based on brain research indicating that teachers should provide many complex and concrete experiences to optimize learning. The brain makes infinite connections among these experiences and thus creates meaningful, long-term learning. Teachers use these methods with students and experience and participate in active interdisciplinary learning themselves.

This curriculum thrives on connections among the disciplines. Science, art, music, drama, language arts, and social studies all focus on the overarching program theme or concept. The purpose of Project SAIL is to develop higher order mental connections and synthesis in an effort to promote both the joy of learning and long-term understanding. This is an intellectual atmosphere in which talents emerge and develop.

In one of Mrs. Abercrombies's writing workshops, Jonathan wrote imaginatively about building a pyramid:

> It is hot. There is nothing as far as the eye can see. The sun is blinding in the hot afternoon sky. We finally came to the ramp. As hot as we are, it seems so impossible. One hour later we made it. Now we have to come back down but it is easier because there is not a rock to carry. When we get to the bottom we get a very little bit of water then we have to go back up the ramp again. By the end of the day some lie on the sand sweating. And some leave for home getting food for the next busy day.

In a writing class with the youngest students, Debi Foster introduced the productive thinking talent on the day the classes studied ancient Egypt. Students had listened to a morning speaker dressed as the Egyptian architect, Imhotep, who talked about the pyramids. Participating teacher Brenda Busby described the class:

> Mrs. Foster related productive thinking to the list of words the students had come up with about their homes. Mrs. Foster wrote the words Egypt, Egyptian, pyramid, and Imhotep on chart paper. She used illustrations from a book about Egypt to give students

some concept of the size of pyramids. The students were then asked to list words that express what they saw or felt in the pyramid. Mrs. Foster told the students to write in their journals using words from the chart or words of their own. She went from table to table discussing words with them and encouraging their writing.

Another of the daily workshops involved interest development centers. The teacher, Melanie Kelsey, introduced the decision-making talent by relating it to the familiar experience of choosing what to wear. Mrs. Kelsey explained the decision-making talent and then guided the students through each of the centers. Students choose their centers and begin to work. One of the participant observers, Judy Miller, described the centers: "The room is filled with centers for each period of architecture. There are pictures, posters, manipulatives, games, activities, and computers to explore." Marilyn Howard had a similar area set up with interest development centers for fourth through sixth graders. A popular computer program in her class is SimCity, in which players have control of planning a city.

In a drama class for kindergarten through third graders, the teacher read a book about castles. A visiting teacher described what happened next:

The teacher guided the students through the planning talent to plan the building of a castle with blocks. She encouraged them to think of the various parts they would need to construct. The students worked well together with leaders emerging. Lots of imagination was used to develop trap doors, drawbridges, and secret rooms.

In a science projects class, Sharon Block had students construct columns and beams and then measure the weight a beam can hold. Another day, she had them compare the weight that a post and lintel system can sustain with that of an arch. In a later class, students built domes. Participant observer Gwen Smith described the day that Mrs. Block had pairs of students build with wet sand and twigs:

Students were drawn in immediately to the task at hand and were busy and involved in the building project. One group built an underground dwelling. Mrs. Block drew out information that the home was structurally sound and that it would be cool in summer and warm in winter like one of the houses about which Laura Ingalls Wilder wrote. Another group had a nest structure, another a tepee, and yet another looked like a Frank Lloyd Wright. The time went by quickly and clean-up came almost too soon.

In consultant Gail Herman's drama classes, students created buildings with their bodies to feel the stress and strain of being a building. In another of her classes, students used songs and instruments to develop a play about Egypt. Teachers observe ways for students to create plays. They will use these strategies when they prepare their students for the Winter Drama Festival.

One culminating event of the summer architectural program was an architectural treasure hunt by bus. Three buses took students and teachers through neighborhoods and downtown to hunt for examples of our architectural past. Students were quick to note rooftops that looked like pyramids, Greek pediments, Roman arches, Gothic spires and arches, Romanesque towers, Renaissance facades, and many neoclassical homes. Following the bus trip, students returned to school to create cities of their own from clay that were videotaped and shown on a local TV station.

## THE SAILS BOOKS

University School teachers wrote a series of books to accompany the SAIL program. The Students' Active Interdisciplinary Learning Series is divided into important historical time periods. The ideals of each of the time periods are revealed through the art, architecture, writing, music, science, math, and history of the era. The books clearly and visually demonstrate how one time period influenced another. The active interdisciplinary learning approach in the SAILS books enables gifted behaviors to emerge.

The purpose of the books is to provide a framework for understanding historical patterns. This framework shows modern-day links to ancient civilizations. The books help students to understand and appreciate the visual heritage that surrounds them. The books demonstrate interdisciplinary active learning and encourage teachers and students to create their own. The following titles have been published, and more are on the way: *Classical Greece, Ancient Rome, The Renaissance, Baroque & Rococo, Neoclassicism,* and *Romanticism.*

## YEAR-ROUND SAIL ACTIVITIES

University School sponsors an annual series of community service events that encourage active interdisciplinary learning and talent development. In addition to the summer SAIL workshops, there are the Fall Parent and Teacher Institute, the Winter Drama Festival, and the Spring Renaissance Fair, which showcases students' and adults' creative products.

### Fall Parent and Teacher Institute

Each fall, leaders in the field of gifted education and parenting education provide workshops, seminars, and lectures at the Parent and Teacher Institute. This 3-day event is sponsored by the University School at the

University of Tulsa. Over the years, a number of groups have supported this event, including the University of Oklahoma Tulsa Medical College, the National Science Foundation, the National Association for Gifted Children (NAGC), the U.S. Department of Education Javits grants, and the Oklahoma Association for Gifted, Creative, and Talented.

Generally, there is an evening meeting just for parents and teachers, a morning keynote session followed by questions and answers that is open to parents and older students, an afternoon of various breakout present- ations for parents, and a Saturday morning of active interdisciplinary learning activities for parents and their children of all ages. The community is invited.

Summer SAIL workshop teachers are accompanied to the institute by their support teams of administrators and parents. The purpose of this aspect of the project is to (a) provide follow-up to the summer workshop; (b) provide professional expertise to teachers, parents, and administrators regarding the needs of gifted students; and (c) help parents, teachers, and administrators feel and be a part of a concerted effort to support their students.

Some of the topics covered at the Parent and Teacher Institute have included the following: underachievement at home and school, stress among the gifted, habits that encourage learning, setting positive expecta- tions, and nurturing talents and gifts. Many of the topics are appropriate for both teachers and the parents. The purpose of the event is to provide information on how to bring out the best in bright students.

## Winter Drama Festival

It usually starts on a cold day in February. If we are lucky, there will be only a little snow on the ground and no ice. On very lucky February morn- ings, it will be clear, sunny, and brisk as the school buses start to open their doors. The first person off the bus may be wearing a Viking helmet with a top hat in one hand and a Greek mask in another. Teachers, parents, and students loaded with theater paraphernalia make their way up the steps of the university student union.

Each year since 1987, students have presented original plays at the Winter Drama Festival sponsored by University School at the University of Tulsa. The plays are usually a class or small group project in which students research, develop, and produce plays under the guidance of a teacher.

The rules for the Winter Drama Festival are simple. All plays must be based on a historic person or event that can be researched. The purpose of this rule is to ensure that some study is involved. Although the play may be inventive and creative, it must be based on research because the purpose of this drama festival is to demonstrate the importance of plays as a method for teaching curriculum content.

The plays must be original creations of a student or group of students under the guidance of a teacher. Teachers need to be involved just as a coach is involved with a team. Without adult guidance, the plays will not be as good as they can be, and the students will not learn enough from the experience.

The content of the plays is finally the decision of the teacher. Ideally, students will have a voice in the decision, but ultimately, the topic and the content must meet with the teacher's approval. Topics have ranged across time and space from ancient Egypt to the modern period. Plays have been about presidents, artists, wars, slavery, dictators, inventions, time periods, local history, and much more. Plays have had elaborate sets, music, and costumes. Plays have been simple, using only human voice with students dressed all in black. They have varied from the boring to the highly entertaining. The teacher must be aware of what makes the difference. It is not costumes, scenery, or music. The teacher's job is that of being an informed and aware coach.

The plays may be no longer than 10 minutes. This limit teaches students and teachers to work within fixed time boundaries. Learning to work within parameters is a good life skill for everyone, particularly for creative and talented people.

In addition to those rules, we encourage teachers to stay clear of overused theme devices such as the "Time Machine." We ask schools not to rely on using a curtain. In a 10-minute play, it is not needed if planned for in advance. We ask the teacher to make sure there is action and movement of characters. A series of monologues can make a boring play. We ask students to speak clearly and project their voices. No matter how wonderful a play is, if it cannot be heard, it will not be successful. Scene changes need to be made swiftly, without causing a break in the flow of the play. All of the above subtleties are the job of the teacher or coach.

At University School, students spend the fall semester in social studies learning about and researching the drama festival topic for that year. One year, the topic was the Civil War. A speaker came and brought Civil War memorabilia that he had found. As part of their own research, students created products and gave presentations. In language arts class, they read Civil War literature and wrote about their responses to it. All this gave students an excellent background and knowledge of the period.

Students have learned that plays must have a conflict or problem. In January, students begin to identify what the problem will be, how it will be introduced, and how it will be resolved. By February, students are down to the details of costumes, timing, and further cutting. By drama festival time, the miracle occurs. The plays spring to life. Entertainment and education become one.

Schools select which performance area they prefer. There is a traditional stage with seating for 400 people and two smaller carpeted rooms where theater-in-the-round or typical theater-style seating can be set up.

We have had as many as 32 schools perform and attend. This means that more than 1,000 people will attend. The festival schedule is generally flexible to accommodate an expanding or shrinking number of schools and performances. When many schools attend, we have plays for 3 full days. If fewer schools come, we have plays for just 3 mornings.

Students and teachers are encouraged to evaluate their own plays and that of others. A form with various criteria is printed in the program. The evaluation covers such things as whether the actors could be heard, whether the play was interesting, and what should be done differently next time.

The Winter Drama Festival has a wide appeal for teachers, students, and their parents. The drama festival provides an excellent vehicle for students' creativity. It helps ensure that students have opportunities for interdisciplinary study and integration of subject matter. At various times, activity packets, theater games, evaluations, and "ice breakers" have been a part of the Winter Drama Festival. The Winter Drama Festival also provides one element of accountability for the teachers involved in the summer workshop. It lets the school administrators and parents see what the students can accomplish.

The plays are a great commitment in both time and effort from students, teachers, and parents. The rewards of satisfaction and learning are immense. Some teachers have been participating for more than a decade because it makes learning enjoyable and memorable. When many things we have done in school are forgotten, the memories of our parts in plays will remain. Students who have been involved in these plays say they are never afraid of speaking in front of an audience or giving a presentation.

### Spring Renaissance Fair

In May, when the buses arrive at the student union, people's arms are loaded with an incredible variety of materials—from computers to fly swatters, from portable showers to wooden sculpture. Hundreds of exhibits of student and adult creative products will miraculously sprout as the minutes pass. The woodcarver is a department chair and professor of pediatrics who has generously given his time over the years to share his hobby with students and adults.

The Renaissance Fair is a 1-day celebration in May of students' and adults' creative products sponsored by University School at the University of Tulsa; the Harmon Foundation also was a sponsor one year. Both students and adults exhibit their creative products while activities encourage participants to interact with the exhibitors. The Renaissance Fair has been a successful way to provide students with an authentic audience for their products. Teachers encourage students to do in-depth research in an area of their interest and create related products to share with other students and adults from around the state and region.

The Renaissance Fair provides another element of accountability for the summer workshop participants. Their students have the opportunity to develop a creative product and exhibit it along with the work of other creative adult and student producers. The purpose of this aspect of the project is to encourage creative products and in-depth studies that are shared with an audience. Administrators and parents accompany students and teachers to this event. Everyone sees the fruits of the active interdisciplinary learning curriculum. Parents see how much students can accomplish; perhaps most important, students see that their creative efforts are valued by their teachers, parents, the school, and the community at large.

## THE NETWORK NEWS QUARTERLY

Since 1986, *The Network News Quarterly* (*NNQ*) has provided teachers, administrators, and parents with information concerning many aspects of gifted education. Topics have included emotional intelligence, styles of parenting, active interdisciplinary learning, NAGC presentations, Kumon math, writing, and the heightened sensitivities of gifted children.

Teachers, parents, and administrators involved in University School programs receive the *NNQ*, which provides the details of components of teacher training programs, plus timely articles concerning the needs of gifted children. The newsletter is the basis for networking among those already involved in University School activities and those who will become involved as a result of their participation in the SAIL project.

## UNIVERSITY SCHOOL

The University School at the University of Tulsa, established in 1982, is a nonprofit educational organization. In addition to the community service described in this chapter, University School provides total school programming for gifted children from age 3 though eighth grade. Although the school is a community service provided by the University of Tulsa, the school's operating budget is based on tuition paid for by the students' parents.

University School, located on the University of Tulsa campus, welcomes visitors and inquiries about the school or its programs. The mailing address is 600 South College Avenue, Tulsa, OK 74104; phone: 918-631-5060; fax: 918-631-5065; Web site: www.uschool@utulsa.edu.

# 9

# *The Prevention and Enrichment Program for Families With Gifted Children*

## *Ruth Erken*

The idea to create the Prevention and Enrichment Program for Families With Gifted Children began when I worked for a German Parents Association for gifted children as a counselor and program coordinator. After some time, I began to recognize a common theme in the problems parents described: Those parents and their friends and acquaintances had little or no information about gifted children and their needs. This made it difficult for them to communicate effectively with their children and also with the school staff, teachers, headmaster, psychologists, and, on a more personal level, neighbors, relatives, and friends.

This is where a complex system of problems has its root. These parents very often feel insecure, misunderstood and distressed, and even sometimes scared because of their special situation. They feel that there is something unusual about their children, but they do not know what it could possibly be. Not only lack of information but also contradictory information about their children distresses parents.

The children often live a sort of double life. At home, they behave like "typical" gifted children: They read books, work with computers and on several different projects, and talk and argue on a mature level. In kindergarten or in school, they may behave quite differently: They are aggressive, refuse any work or play, are very shy and scared, and refuse much contact with the other children.

This is not unusual to most of the readers who work in the field of gifted education and know these problems well. But most of the parents I have known in a counseling capacity had never heard of some of the complex behaviors associated with giftedness. They tended to believe in the widespread myth that gifted children are those who have the best marks in class, experience success in any field they work in, and need no special advice or support.

These parents accepted the conclusions of the nursery or elementary school teachers that their children are emotionally and behaviorally disturbed or simply troublemakers. They never suspected giftedness. Under this misunderstanding and the stress that often accompanies it, communication becomes difficult and is more likely to create new problems and misunderstandings. In some cases, children develop serious emotional disturbance, behavioral, and psychosomatic disorders such as diffuse pain in several parts of the body, depression, auto-aggressive behavior, stomach ulcers, and suicidal thoughts.

This is the point where those not well informed about gifted children may believe in another widespread myth about them—namely, that gifted children are emotionally unstable. Although this myth may appear justified in some cases, the following question remains: What is cause and what is effect? Put another way, do the problems experienced by gifted children come from the children themselves or from the situation around them?

## GIFTED EDUCATION IN GERMANY

I want to add a few sentences about the German situation with regard to the support of gifted children. There are two parent associations for gifted children in Germany and some counseling centers connected with psychological or educational institutes at universities that include researchers who specialize in the field of giftedness. Another organization is Bildung und Begabung, the German office of ECHA (European Council for High Ability), which also coordinates extracurricular activities such as summer academies.

Furthermore, there are several competitions in different subjects for pupils. The most famous are *Jugend forscht* and *Jugend musiziert*. The first competition is meant for innovations in the field of science and technology, and the second is a competition for young musicians in the field of classical music. There are also competitions ("Olympic games") for pupils in chemistry, mathematics, physics, foreign languages, recent history, and so on. These competitions are annual. The problem is that only those pupils gain access to these competitions whose teachers know about them and who support the pupils' projects. The competitions are designed for pupils at the secondary school level.

When taking a serious look at the situation in Germany, one must conclude that gifted education plays the role of the outsider in the field of education generally. The lecturers at the university and teachers' training seminars only seldom consider the topic of giftedness. Few psychologists established in private practice are interested in the needs of gifted children in addition to their work with other clients. Consequently, parents lack opportunities to inform themselves about the common behaviors and characteristics of gifted children and their special needs.

Because the counseling centers are connected with universities, many parents are hesitant to come into contact with university teachers, especially if they have no academic background. As a result, most parents with gifted children first learn about giftedness when their own children are in serious trouble at school or in kindergarten. Some parents whom I got to know as a counselor were in a desperate situation because of the psychological disorders of their children such as depression, isolation, aggressive outbursts, and, in some extreme cases, suicidal thoughts and behavior.

Because the majority of teachers and other professionals know little about the special needs of gifted children, the families whom bring their problems to a counselor tend to be those who have little choice; they face a situation that has reached a critical point or has a long developmental history. In no way do the participants in the Prevention and Enrichment Program for Families With Gifted Children represent the whole population, although they may express similar needs and tendencies. Although it makes little sense to generalize from these families' situations, all parents face similar challenges when it comes to supporting the unique abilities of their gifted children.

Another important influence on gifted education in Germany lies in recent German history, especially political and social history. The concept of elitism is closely connected with the topic of giftedness and the support of gifted youth. This concept of elitism was part of the fascist ideology of the Nazis, who restricted the term *elite* to a self-appointed group of people who adopted a racist ideology. Because of the rise of Nazism (1933-1945), the term *elitism,* with its hidden connotation, has become restricted to this ideological meaning. This dark period in German history was traumatic for the German postwar generation. The whole society, the political system, and especially the education system had to be renewed.

The idea was to begin with the education system because that is where the future of Germany lies and where the generations to come would bring hope for profound changes in the political attitude of a people. The idea of equal opportunity for all children, regardless of their social background, became a fundamental goal in German education. Naturally, this ideal is valuable and important in a democratic society. The problem is the present tendency to see a contradiction between the ideal of equality of opportunity for all children (with special regard to those who come from a working-class background) and the adequate support of gifted children. The fear of producing a new uncontrollable group of people—a new elite with all its negative connotations—is very strong.

Most people think that gifted people are privileged by nature and that society does not need to offer them even more privileges. Of course, this is a mistaken and shortsighted view. In my opinion, the education of gifted youth should help children to become responsible and mature members of society, able to use their intellectual capacities for invention and improvement in any field. Gaining the education and support they need will enable them to give back to society their enormous richness of ideas and inventions in science, the arts, politics, and business.

On the other hand, ignoring and excluding the needs of gifted youth often leads to isolation and psychological disorders as described previously. The latter could lead to gifted persons who have no caring and courage at all (Webb, 1995). Some of those neglected are in danger of misusing their intellectual capacity for criminal and destructive acts or schemes. The question that again rises up is as follows: What is cause and what is effect?

## PREVENTION

First, I would like to give some background on prevention in a theoretical or scientific context. *Prevention,* as defined by Caplan (1964), could be divided into the following:

- Primary prevention
- Secondary prevention
- Tertiary prevention

This concept may seem vague, but in this context it should be understood as follows:

- Primary prevention means that the prevention starts before a psychological disorder can be developed.
- Secondary prevention refers to early diagnosis of a disorder and the prevention of other disorders that result from the first one.
- Tertiary prevention means that a psychological disorder has already developed in a person, but coping strategies to live with this disorder without being severely handicapped can be learned.

In the context of the Prevention and Enrichment Program for Families With Gifted Children, the focus lies on primary and secondary prevention. This is important because this program is only created for families who are stable and who have a close and satisfactory relationship with one another, not for those families who find themselves in an acute crisis or who have developed serious and chronic psychosomatic disorders (such as alcohol or drug abuse, suicidal behavior of one or more members of the family, psychosis, depression, or any other serious disorder).

The latter sort of families with gifted children should be given the strong advice to undergo medical treatment. The major issue in those families is, of course, not the giftedness of one of their children but the serious mental health status of the whole family system. This prevention program cannot provide the kind of care and support such a family would need. It is intended to serve families who are interested in becoming informed about the common behaviors and characteristics of giftedness and the special needs of their gifted children. The program focuses on the development of family communication skills as a means of ensuring the normal growth of gifted children and the well-being of the family as a whole. It should be seen as an enrichment and resource program, not as a treatment for ill persons.

## PREVENTION AND ENRICHMENT PROGRAM FOR FAMILIES WITH GIFTED CHILDREN

This program is based on the Parent Effectiveness Training (PET) by Gordon (1970). The main difference between PET and this program is the special target group—namely, those families with gifted children. Another point is that this program is more structured than we usually find in the programs of L'Abate (see L'Abate & Weinstein, 1987) and other more behaviorist authors and researchers in the field. My experience in working with groups of families, especially those with preschool and elementary school children for whom the program is designed, shows that it makes sense to work with a more structured program. At best, a laxity in structure often fails to address the specific issues families most need help on; at worst, it can put gifted children and their families at risk of even greater misunderstanding and miscommunication.

## OUTLINE OF THE PROGRAM FOR PARENTS

1.   At first, the counselor who comes into contact with the parents in a counseling center invites parents to participate in the program. A brochure that contains some information on the purpose and aim of the program would be helpful.

2.   The counselor makes a note of those parents who show interest in participating in the program.

3.   The counselor engages interested parents in an introductory conversation to get to know the family better and to gather some background information on them. This conversation is meant to find out if the family fits into the context and conception of the program or if they need another kind of support system for their situation. If the counselor finds out that the family suffers from a serious psychological and psychosomatic disorder, he or she could help them find the kind of professional help they need in this particular case (either a clinical psychologist, a psychiatrist, or another professional who could be a resource person to them).

4.   After this conversation, the counselor should register those families who fit the design and conception of the program and offer two books to them as an introduction to the field of gifted children: *Guiding the Gifted Child (Hochbegabte Kinder* in the German version), by James Webb, Elizabeth Meckstroth, and Stephanie Tolan (1982), and *Our Child Is Gifted: A Guide for Parents and Teachers (Unser Kind ist hochbegabt: Ein Leitfaden für Eltern und Lehrer)*, by Franz Monks and Irene Ypenburg (1993). The parents read these two books to prepare themselves for the first part of the program. The program is designed for four to six families and includes six meetings altogether (including one weekend).

The first meeting takes place on a weekend, from Friday evening to Sunday afternoon, in an educational institution combining conference rooms and a hostel. This compact meeting is meant to offer families the possibility to get to know each other and to establish contact between the parents and the children who are in similar situations. On Friday evening, the families check into their rooms. All families, as well as the supervisor and his or her assistant, have dinner together. The assistant must be a person experienced in the field of gifted education, and he or she will be the supervisor of the children's program. Of course, there must be activities appropriate for gifted preschool and elementary school children. Saturday is a resource day. The supervisor introduces himself or herself as well as the supervisor of the children's program.

## A PHILOSOPHY PROGRAM FOR THE CHILDREN

A philosophy program for the children is useful because it relates to the content of the parents' program (communication, reflection on basic questions) and because many gifted children begin to ask how the world works from an early age. They reflect on questions such as, "What is time? How do people differ from animals? How does evil come into the world?" Even at the preschool age, gifted children ponder philosophical questions, which are often regarded as extremely abstract and theoretical.

While the supervisor deals with the parents, the assistant gathers the children and helps them to introduce themselves. This might be a chance to encourage the children to ask the kinds of questions that are mentioned above. Through a variety of activities, the assistant shows the children how great philosophers approach these important questions. She or he and the children explore the history and development of philosophy through prepared pictures (e.g., photos of Greek statues, paintings of great philosophers), biographies, and other written information. The assistant guides the discussion around five philosophical topics so that the children can talk to one another:

1. *Logic.* This topic deals with the rules of thinking. A typical philosopher in this context is Aristotle. The supervisor and children focus on his biography and his style of thinking; the children also get simple but characteristic costumes so that they can play Aristotle teaching his followers. In the same way, the group explores the other four topics.

2. *Epistemology.* The supervisor of the children's program talks with the children about their senses (sight, hearing, smell, taste, touch) and especially about how the subjectivity and objectivity of perception influence the construction of reality. The leading question here is as follows: Is it possible to know what is going on in the world outside of ourselves? The philosopher who reflected on this question is René Descartes.

3. *Theory of Science.* This topic deals with the question of how one gains ideas and cognitions in certain fields of science. Socrates should be mentioned because of his so-called "What is" questions—What is good? What is bravery? What is a human being? This leads to discourse theory that relates to the kind of questions young gifted children ask.

4. *Ethics.* This topic is about how to live a good and moral life, how to become a "good human being," and, in general, about good and evil. This is important for young children who have just begun to reflect on basic questions of morality. The philosopher being introduced in this context is Immanuel Kant. His four principal questions are mentioned and explained:

1. What can I know? (*Was kann ich wissen?*)

2. What am I to do? (*Was soll ich tun?*)

3. What am I allowed to hope? (*Was darf ich hoffen?*)

4. What is man supposed to be? (*Was ist der Mensch?*)

The last question is the basic philosophical question that leads to all other philosophical questions.

5. *Metaphysics.* This last topic deals with things beyond nature. For instance, Does God exist? What is the meaning of life? Is there something

beyond mere matter? What is behind physics? The children usually get some religious education (in Germany, usually Christian) from their parents as well as in kindergarten or elementary school. The supervisor introduces Thomas of Aquino to the children, a famous philosopher who reflected on the question of God. The children have the option of playing the roles of the philosophers and their followers. They wear costumes and develop a philosophical drama.

On Saturday, the children work on the philosophical program, the draft of the script, and rehearsals. On Sunday, they perform for the parents. Each child gets a photo of himself or herself playing a philosopher, as well as a brochure synthesizing the knowledge and ideas they learned and used in the course of the program. In this way, both the parents and the children have something to take home. My intention is that this will stimulate many discussions between the parents and their gifted children.

## THE PARENT PROGRAM

I will now turn to the parents' part of the weekend seminar. Both supervisors act on Saturday as resource persons. This means that the supervisors do not give a prepared lecture but show interest in the questions that arise during the reading of the books about gifted children or the handouts in the children's program. The supervisor should prepare a catalog of generic terms in the field of giftedness as well as some of the typical problems parents have. This catalog of generic terms includes the following:

1. Definitions of giftedness

2. Identification of gifted children

3. Giftedness in society

4. Gifted children and their peers

5. Gifted children in kindergarten and at school
   (a) Overachievement
   (b) Underachievement

6. Extracurricular activities for gifted children

7. Gifted children at home and with their siblings

8. Gifted children and depression and other psychological dysfunctions

9. The prospects of gifted children

All these generic terms should be written down on the blackboard or on an overhead projector. Parents can also supplement this catalog if they find important points missing. The catalog of generic terms is meant to be a connecting thread that can provide a structure for the questions the parents ask and for discussion. This structure also puts the broad range of questions and issues that come up in some kind of manageable order so that parents can decide what they would like to know.

It is important to have a structure for the discussion because it keeps the discussions from becoming circuitous and confusing. Otherwise, new information comes to the parents in chaos, and in the end, no one knows which answer was given to which question. The supervisor acts as a facilitator who leads the discussion, taking care that the questions fit in the sequence of the generic terms. He or she also ensures that everyone has the freedom to ask questions and that the session be fruitful and open within its structure. The discussion starts after breakfast, breaks for lunch, and then goes on until dinner. After dinner, there will be time for voluntary activities.

On Sunday, the supervisor introduces the parents to PET in its specified version, along with the background and conception of it. The central idea of PET in its specified version for families with gifted children is that parents should avoid any force in their education of and interaction with their children. The parents learn different ways to interact and communicate with their children in a relationship that is based on partnership. According to Gordon (1970), it is important for the parents to learn to avoid 12 typical mistakes in their interactions with their children:

1. Ordering, directing, commanding

2. Warning, admonishing, threatening

3. Exhorting, moralizing, preaching

4. Advising, giving solutions or suggestions

5. Lecturing, teaching, giving logical arguments

6. Judging, criticizing, disagreeing, blaming

7. Praising, agreeing

8. Name-calling, ridiculing, shaming

9. Interpreting, analyzing, diagnosing

10. Reasoning, sympathizing, consoling, supporting

11. Probing, questioning, interrogating

12. Withdrawing, distracting, humoring, diverting

Some of the "typical" 12 communication mistakes may seem surprising, such as reasoning and supporting, but all of them can, in certain contexts, create communication barriers. According to Gordon (1970), they can express a hierarchical relationship between parent and child. These messages convey the parents' nonacceptance. It is a learning process to avoid the 12 typical communication mistakes and demands a fundamental change in the parents' attitude toward their children. The parents learn to accept their children just the way they are. This does not mean that if they do so, the children remain as they are and there is no constructive development. This change in the interactive style of the parents enables them to practice the "no-lose method" successfully.

This short description of the main aim and purpose of the program demonstrates why PET is especially appropriate for families with gifted children. I have learned from experience that families with gifted children have a higher need for communication. This is a direct result of the giftedness. A lot of decisions have to be made by the parents if they have a gifted child, especially in the preschool and elementary school years. These decisions carry weight because of their influence on the child's future development and quality of life.

Examples of these decisions include the following: Which school is the best school for a gifted child? Maybe a boarding school with special classes for gifted children, but far away from home? What about boarding schools abroad? Or would it be better to stay in the school around the corner so that the child has a familiar social environment, his or her friends in the neighborhood, and enough free time for several projects? Should the parents send their children for an IQ test, or are the children in danger of becoming arrogant and spoiled if the results prove that they are gifted? Should children skip a grade in school? What consequences could result from grade skipping? What sort of extracurricular activities should the parents allow their children? Is the computer the right sort of activity? Should the young children learn foreign languages at an early age, or are they at risk of being so far ahead of their classmates that they become isolated?

All these questions and many more become acute in preschool and elementary school, where decisions can have a strong impact on the child's development and quality of life. This is the point in life when decisions can either enable a child to grow and expand or disable him or her. Because the educational system is designed for the needs of children with average intelligence, any child who performs below or above that average becomes a minority. Any sort of minority status can potentially cause problems because of the social isolation that minorities suffer at the hands of the majority.

This makes the situation difficult for the parents who find themselves torn between conforming to the system and rebelling against it. Therefore, it makes more sense to prepare the parents, and of course the children, for the kind of challenges they will have to face. The best way to prepare them is to inform them extensively and to help them develop their communication ability with their children and the school so that they can resolve problems before they become serious. Knowledge about giftedness and skill in communication will be needed in many situations when parents have to find their own way and discover innovative or unique solutions for their child. Often, the parents find themselves alone in dealing with a difficult situation, and they have to trust their own power of judgment.

With regard to the parents' program, it is sensible to divide the seminar meetings into topics that address common issues and problems faced by parents of gifted children.

First meeting topic: language of acceptance
 Passive listening
 Active listening

Second meeting topic: "I messages".

Third meeting topic: changing unacceptable behavior by changing the environment

Fourth meeting topic: the no-lose method

Fifth and final meeting topic: résumé and evaluation of the program by the parents; farewell ceremony and informal pleasant evening

The meetings are structured as follows: The supervisor explains the conception and background of the topics and gives an example of a typical conversation with a gifted child. It could be an example from everyday life or one concerning a difficult decision, as long as it occurs often in families with gifted children so that the parents can identify with it.

Then there should be an opportunity to pick up examples that occur often in the parents' families. Next, the parents try to see a problem from a different perspective, using the background of their new knowledge about an interaction based on partnership. After that, the supervisor tells the parents about the risks of the methods because, otherwise, they could be misunderstood as a sort of laissez-faire education.

## 1. First Meeting Topic: Language of Acceptance

The basic issue here is that a person must be able to feel and communicate genuine acceptance for another human being. Many parents think that acceptance does not preclude them from molding their child's development. They think that if they wish the child to make a constructive change or any further development, all they need to do is to communicate in the language of nonacceptance, such as criticism.

At this point, the supervisor needs to explain why the acceptance of parents has such a positive influence on the children. The language of nonacceptance creates the risk of self-fulfilling prophecy. For example, if one tells the child often enough that she or he is disorganized, the child may become disorganized and even may, out of rebellion, defend this disorganization. In addition to the danger of self-fulfilling prophecy, the language of nonacceptance also suggests to a child that his or her parents do not love the child *as he or she is.* This feeling that many gifted children harbor—that they are unacceptable as they are—is one of the most hurtful and can severely handicap a sensitive child.

The unspoken as well as spoken messages that attend the language of nonacceptance demonstrate the necessity for parents to show their acceptance. Specific skills are required to be able to do this, such as passive and active listening.

*Passive listening* means more than just being silent. This sounds simple, but passive listening is a strong nonverbal message that communicates acceptance. For example, a child thinks she cannot explain to her parents her mixed feelings about skipping a grade. She starts to tell them, but the parents stay silent and just listen to the child without criticizing or interrupting out of fear that the child could make the wrong decision. Acceptance in this case means sympathizing with the child and her current situation and not jumping to their own concerns about the child's future. The risk of passive listening lies in the fact that a child could misinterpret being silent as not being interested in what the child is saying.

*Active listening* is a concept that comes from the therapeutic setting of Rogers's client-centered psychotherapy. Active listening means that the parents decode the children's feelings—understand their message and put this into their own words. It does not mean sending a message themselves but simply expressing verbally how they understand their children's feelings. By checking with their children to be sure the message is accurate, parents will avoid misunderstandings. For example, a child feels unaccepted by classmates because he is not very good at sports:

> Child:    "I wish I could play football as the others can."
> Father:   "You feel you are not good at sports."
> Child:    "Yes."

The risk in this communication is that the parents might inadvertently express their own rather than their child's messages, and this would be the language of nonacceptance.

### 2. Second Meeting: Language of Acceptance

The topic for this meeting is "I messages" and "you messages." "I messages" and "you messages" are two different ways of confrontation. In everyday life, parents tend to use "you messages" if they want to express their own feelings or attitude about the child's behavior. For example, a child is making a loud noise (e.g., playing the trumpet to gain attention). The parent says, "You are naughty. You shouldn't be so loud." What the parent really means is, "I cannot relax if there is such a loud noise around." "You messages" are ineffective because they don't convey the parents' real feelings—namely, that the loud music disturbs the parents' peace and concentration. "I messages" are much more effective in modifying a child's behavior because they are more truthful and avoid the vicious circle of mutual accusation.

The risk with these two different confrontational messages is that when parents start giving "I messages," they may be ignored by the children. After having been ignored a few times, the parents return to "you messages" and dismiss the "I messages" as ineffective. It is important that they should not give up so quickly but convey their "I messages" more intensively.

## 3. Third Meeting: Changing Unacceptable Behavior by Changing the Environment

This means that the parents can change the child's unacceptable behavior by modifying the surroundings. This is a typical problem most parents of gifted children know: Gifted children typically immerse themselves in projects scattered from the attic to the basement of the house, leaving a mess. This of course leads to an endless and tiresome discussion about "the untidy child."

Gordon (1970) suggested eight different possibilities to change the surroundings of the child:

1. Enriching the environment

2. Impoverishing it

3. Simplifying it

4. Restricting it

5. Childproofing it

6. Substituting one activity for another

7. Preparing the child for changes in his environment

8. Planning ahead with older children

In practice, parents could do the following:

1. Enriching the environment: They could supply their children's rooms with sufficient materials, games, and so forth, so that they no longer need to use other rooms.

2. Impoverishing it: They provide rooms in the household that are restricted to certain activities (e.g., the living room or the child's

bed). These places should not be enriched but should serve as quiet places.

3. Simplifying it: They can change the environment to make it easier for the child to function. The environment should give the child a clear working area, easy access to supplies and cleanup, and be age and ability appropriate.

4. Restricting it: The areas where the child can play are limited to the child's room, other rooms conducive to child activities, or outside.

5. Childproofing it: They can put everything dangerous away from the child, such as sharp knives.

6. Substituting one activity for another: If the child plays with things that are dangerous for him or her, parents should substitute them with less dangerous objects that also hold interest for the child.

7. Preparing the child for changes in the environment: If there will be changes in the household, inform the child in time for him or her to think it over and get used to the idea.

8. Planning ahead with other children: Parents' acceptance should grow and develop with all the children in the family.

Teenagers have needs for privacy and independent activities that are different from children, and parents should change some things to show that they accept this maturing process (e.g., always knocking before entering the teenager's room). The risk here is that in some areas, it may be hard to convince parents to modify the household, especially if they cannot see the need and feel restricted in their own home. In this case, the best approach has been to encourage gradual modifications or compromises to see if they make a difference to the child.

## 4. Fourth Meeting: The No-Lose Method

Most parents are used to thinking in terms of winning or losing. Encouraged by society, this attitude dominates sports competitions as well as competitions in school for the best marks and so on. Because of this, parents lack the skill to negotiate compromises and tend to believe that a situation in which no one wins and no one loses is in reality a loss in disguise.

Looking into democratic society, one finds important fields where compromises are common, such as a negotiation between a union and the head of a company about higher wages or negotiations for a coalition between two parties after an election. Our political culture has established an egalitarian relationship between two parties whose needs are different so that fair negotiations can proceed. These kinds of negotiations for an acceptable compromise are what is meant by a no-lose method.

As the two examples above show, it makes sense to educate children to participate fully in a democratic society—and that includes the democratic process in everyday life. The advantage is that the children learn to think through their point of view carefully and learn how to negotiate for their own interests in a reasonable and responsible way. This method is especially appropriate for gifted children because of their superior thinking style and intellectual capacity. The risk is that parents often assume that it is too cumbersome to negotiate for every decision, and so they often go back to the authoritarian (win-or-lose) method. As a solution to this, families could establish some sort of golden rules that everyone in the household accepts but that allow enough room for negotiations when needed.

## 5. Fifth and Final Meeting

First, the supervisor gives a short summary of the whole Prevention and Enrichment Program for Families With Gifted Children so that the parents have a last review. Then the supervisor distributes a brochure that contains the short overview of the program and all the methods and communication skills so that the parents can read through it again.

After that, the participants will evaluate the program. The parents receive a handout, which they use to evaluate the structure of the program, the supervisor, and their personal success in learning new communication skills and strategies. A possibility for follow-up evaluations could include the parents writing a diary about their experiences with the program or doing several qualitative interviews over a period of time. This sort of evaluation can generate more detailed information and insight that will be useful to the future development of the program.

# CONCLUSION

Families with gifted children are not at higher risk of developing mental health disorders because of their children's giftedness. But these families do need to develop effective ways to communicate with their children. For children in preschool and elementary school, important decisions have to be made. This is why those families with gifted preschool and elementary school children seem to be the best target group for the program. This is a point in the children's lives when parents can avoid serious problems resulting from misguided decisions.

Parents should never be blamed for their decisions; rather, they should be empowered to communicate with their children in a way that brings beneficial results for both parents and children (Gordon, 1970). In my opinion, it is very important to prepare parents for difficulties that can arise with their gifted children and also with the world outside. The best way to do this is first to provide comprehensive information so that parents can discuss and explain the concept of giftedness to important persons such as the nursery school teacher, the school teacher, the school psychologist, other parents, and so on. When parents discuss their concerns from a more informed position, they feel much more secure in the negotiation process than if they know relatively little about giftedness. Parents and children will often find themselves in situations where they must rely on their own power of judgment. The communication skills introduced and developed in this program can be a strong foundation for creating the best solution for a problem.

# 10

# *Role of Programs*

### *Relationships With Parents, Schools, and Communities*

#### *Maria Lucia Sabatella*

At the dawn of a new century and perhaps of a different civilization, educators have called their own values and their pedagogical action into question. Because they have witnessed the immense scientific and technological changes that have influenced society and because they hold human life in great esteem, educators tend to pursue innovative approaches to teaching.

The field of education actually poses some of the greatest challenges today, both to society at large and to the individual. There is much recent research on the nature of humankind and its choices at a time when sophisticated technology keeps increasing the pace and speed of production. Such a state of affairs calls for the development of creative potential, as people seek new alternatives to improve the quality of life. An urgent need exists for research emphasizing new methods of education that shall respond to the advances of science and the demand for optimized learning.

When education is viewed as a global process in society, particularly involving the school and the family, it faces a major challenge in establishing a communication link. We appear to be taking the first steps toward a new age in education and are trying to analyze what kind of teaching will be offered to the generation that will construct the future and keep up with the fast pace of technological change. Schools will make it a point to offer the best education available for every student (Feldhusen & Moon, 1992). As a result, the improvement of knowledge regarding the self and personal growth has become vital. As a consequence, research about giftedness has also expanded. How do individuals learn to make choices, observe, and act spontaneously? How do they cope with challenge, take risks, and develop all of their strengths and talents? How do they become aware of their potential and achievement?

Educators and schools will have to change their points of view and allow for learning experiences that are compatible with current social and technological transformations. Drawing on state-of-the-art research, this chapter reflects on the nature of such a new educational model and how it should be run to help special individuals and students in general achieve their fullest potential as human beings.

The special setting of my pedagogic experience has been Brazil. Although the majority of sources I have reviewed are North American, this chapter focuses on general principles of education for gifted and talented students that may apply to programs worldwide.

## THE ISSUE OF IDENTIFICATION

All research efforts in the field of human behavior concur in recognizing giftedness as a special feature that can be developed when identified accurately. As it is known, intelligence tests are not a conclusive means of identification and are merely one of the instruments used. Students need to be identified on the basis of various methods. Many potentially gifted students are forgotten because they were never included in the early selection process.

The identification of gifted students is a process through which we try to know students whose abilities, motivational patterns, self-esteem, and creative drive are beyond average to the point that they demand different services to develop their potential. All the types of gifts and talents actually correspond to psychological characteristics and abilities that vary continuously. The characteristics exist at various levels in all human beings, but they vary in intensity from person to person. Abilities also differ among the gifted. The process of identification must, therefore, account for these variables (Feldhusen & Baska, 1985).

In addition to the formal processes, we rely on the contribution of two important agents in the primary identification of children with a high potential: teachers and parents. The indication by the teacher is one of the most important and consistent methods. However, the efficacy of identification by the teacher is limited and must be combined with other means, by teachers who have some experience and expertise in the identification of gifted students and are aware of the behavioral characteristics that signal their potential.

Parents have a mine of knowledge and information that may contribute to the child's identification. They know much about the abilities, motivations, self-esteem, and creative drive of their children. Parents also observe behavior in diverse situations, in addition to witnessing the daily homework routine, which is often restricted and inadequate for the child's development. They are aware of gifts and needs frequently invisible to teachers and may be invaluable for a more comprehensive identification.

The role of family, school, and community at an early state is, therefore, crucial for the identification and education of students with great ability or potential. The family must learn how to support and nurture their children's development by seeking more information about giftedness, as well as adequate technical and professional assistance. The school will need to adjust itself to the unique abilities and educational needs of their gifted students. They should begin by overcoming the prejudice that is still found among educators; in addition, there must be effective methods for identifying and recognizing students' potential. The community will need to be informed to foster sociability and the development of students. The more welcome they feel, the sooner they will become leaders who are aware of their capacity and of the challenges ahead.

## THE RELATIONSHIP WITH PARENTS

The family has a crucial role in the individual's upbringing, especially in the affective domain, in the development of positive self-esteem, values, attitudes, interests, and motivations. As Passow (1992) pointed out, family life is the child's first school.

Professionals who design special programs know that it is important to integrate family into their work. The relationship with the families is meant to unify thought and action between parents and teachers. Understanding the students' developmental stages and their needs will be achieved if mutual awareness exists. Working with parents on the discovery and growth of children's special abilities should always be a dimension of a gifted program.

Although rewarding, the role of parents in their children's lives is manifold and incredibly difficult. They are providers, educators and tutors, intellectual and social models, disciplinarians, advisers, listeners, planners, managers, interpreters, authorities, and companions. They foster special interests and talents and act as vocational counselors.

According to Ehrlich (1989), parents may have a constructive or destructive influence on the lives of their children, depending on (a) their own perception of the role that they perform; (b) their ability, knowledge, and background; and (c) their motivations and aspirations. Hackney (1981) presented conclusions of his research on the nature of interaction patterns in families of gifted people and verified that parents and their lifestyles are greatly affected by the presence of a gifted child.

The successful rearing of gifted children depends, to a great extent, on family involvement, particularly in the case of younger children. Children need emotional stability, and they are able to work through challenges more successfully in homes where warmth, affection, and understanding prevail.

Parents of children with high potential have a great need to communicate with other families and exchange experiences with those facing similar issues. Parents of talented children have much in common, but the opportunities to share their family experiences are few because they feel isolated and cannot talk freely to family, neighbors, and friends. Communication with parents of average children is also difficult because they find it hard to understand or even believe information about giftedness.

Many parents quickly learn to downplay their gifted children's behavior as a result of misinformation. Parents often feel stressed living with a child with an insatiable curiosity, intense sensitivity, and a high level of energy. They also verify a discrepancy between the procedures that are recommended for upbringing and the reality that they find in the daily routine with their children. Webb and DeVries (1993) have pointed out that one of the greatest difficulties is that they find few professionals, even at schools, who can offer specific information about gifted education or who are willing to spend time for the kind of guidance required. As a consequence, parents of gifted children often suppress their need to talk about their experiences.

Keeping these communication constraints in mind, program designers should create opportunities for advising and involving family in colloquia, meetings, conferences, and group work so that parents may share experiences, talk about their efforts, and become collaborators and facilitators in talent development. It is essential to create a cooperative atmosphere and to be open to suggestions and collaboration. As time goes by, many parents will begin helping the advising groups, and their participation as tutors may be fostered.

Parents have special expectations from their gifted children's teachers and are very perceptive about what goes on in the programs. These parents notice results in the areas where teachers are focusing, particularly if they are aware of the proposed activity objectives. Their participation and information will also be important for the process of program evaluation.

The school environment alone is not enough to ensure stimulation and development of gifted potential. The importance of family support has been the subject of much research with significant results. Involving parents harmonizes the interests shared by family and school and ensures the complete development of talented children.


## THE RELATIONSHIP WITH TEACHERS

The school has various degrees of responsibility in several aspects of the student's development: intellectual, social, emotional, moral, and physical. The majority of opportunities to broaden the scope of talent are also found at school. The educators' job is to create a stimulating environment that will make it easier for students to develop and explore all of their potential. Educators also act as the discoverers of talent and must be concerned with the students' total development.

During regular classes, students with high ability normally are frustrated by the limitations of their curriculum. They feel a need for more information, greater depth of content, and more varied resources. They are eager to leave the traditional classroom's restrictive routine and take part in extracurricular activities that often provide the only opportunities for them to work at their own pace. They may do their tasks more freely in arts homework, in sport performance, and in library activities without having to wait for the other students. Few gifted students, however, find their regular classes challenging or instructive.

The role of special programs is to fill the gap in the regular education of gifted students and open a space for the broad development of abilities and talents, creating opportunities for them to meet new challenges and find answers. Educators who work in programs for the gifted know that to help these students, they must work with their schools.

Ideally, every teacher should have specific information in the field of special education–focused giftedness. Regular classroom teachers have had to commit themselves to the great responsibility of meeting the affective and cognitive needs of gifted students. They need information about basic procedures of identification and special strategies in this area. Such teachers struggle because of their lack of knowledge and expertise. If they had experience in this field, they would certainly be able to recommend and send gifted students identified in their classes to an adequate service.

Even when the school does not offer specific programs for gifted students, it should have information about basic processes of identification, as well as teacher training in strategies that help recognize special talents and abilities. Teachers may notice gifted behaviors in more students when correct strategies are used. The effective combination of adequate strategies will contribute both to the discovery of talents and to the stimulation and development of all students.

The general objective of educators who are concerned with special needs should be to foster all students' talents according to their ability. Other actions could help fulfill this goal: organizing programs that maintain a relationship with schools, encouraging them to set high educational standards, and helping parents to support their children so that they fully pursue their talents and abilities. Teachers of the gifted have the responsibility and power to change the educational standards for students in general.

Having learned how to use new and innovative teaching methods to challenge high-ability students, educators will acquire more effective techniques for improving and enriching their pedagogical knowledge as a whole. As a consequence, all students will benefit. Johnson (1989) actually argued that education in general changes for the better when practice involving a few students is improved. Good teaching is beneficial not only in programs for the gifted. When a school has to reconsider its curriculum to include activities that stimulate the high-level thinking for the gifted, the curriculum undergoes a complete reexamination.

Therefore, the analysis of research about strategies and methodology applied to gifted education may improve education for all students. New approaches to grouping learners and programming activities will lead to opportunities for everyone to participate in different and advanced classes, designed to meet individual learning needs.

Gifted students demand teacher excellence, and this excellence has a positive impact on all students. The improvement of gifted education is likely to stimulate the future generation as a whole and foster the development of better professionals in all areas of human knowledge.

## THE RELATIONSHIP WITH SCHOOLS

Although some schools already have programs for gifted students in their curricula, the great majority of schools do not even have a system of identification that might qualify students for a special program. Parents and educators often make the mistake of believing that tests and other measuring instruments will provide conclusive results in the identification of a gifted child. We commonly hear parents and teachers wonder whether a particular child who seems brilliant and precocious is actually gifted.

As a result of the difficulties involved in ensuring an accurate identification, special programs cannot be reserved only for gifted students. We must increase the possibilities of access and also draw on the finding of recent research about intelligence to conceive models that reach all students, particularly those who need qualitatively different learning.

Programs designed for the gifted and talented should have a broad and flexible admission system so that opportunities are offered to highly motivated students with talent in specific areas to develop their potential. Motivation sometimes becomes more important than potential and may lead to the appearance of abilities not identified previously.

Planning a program for the gifted that meets the real needs of the students, the parents' expectations, and the educational philosophy of community schools without creating problems in the daily functioning of regular education is a challenge. The goal must be to adjust the students' personal and academic situation to their learning needs and offer all the means available to fully develop their gifts.

Support programs for students with high potential face certain constraints in the regular school system. Gifted children, unlike average children, have two sets of peers: age peers and intellectual peers. It is difficult to try to design special programs in the regular school setting where existing groups are separated by age and not necessarily by intellectual level. When gifted students are placed in special programs, they work with intellectual peers in a learning environment where individual characteristics and needs are respected. As they continue attending regular school, on the other hand, their interaction with peers of the same age group becomes a constraint on their abilities.

Taking into account the difficulties involved in carrying out enrichment programs in the classroom, it has been considered more practicable to undertake these programs by means of extra-class activities and learning centers, where students with special aptitudes organize themselves in groups and participate in activities that meet their interests and abilities. It is crucial for the student to have freedom to choose the subjects that he or she wishes to learn, the scope and depth of study, and his or her favorite learning styles. Thus, the role of the teacher is that of a facilitator in identifying and designing appropriate learning activities and projects, as well as a research adviser (de Alencar, 1986).

One of the most debatable topics has been the improvement of learning alternatives for gifted students. Which instructional conditions are ideal for these students to develop the motivation and interest to achieve excellence at a high level and pursue their goals? Educators who design and administer programs for the gifted and talented must face these crucial issues (Feldhusen & Moon, 1992).

An appraisal of the results of group work has brought illuminating contributions and revealed the advantages of student interaction. Data from genetic social psychology, for example, in studies by Perret-Clermont (1978), indicate that in specific situations, social interaction processes may bring about changes in the individual's cognitive structure.

Research about operational learning also shows that the performance of children who work in small groups during math exercises is qualitatively superior, with the children arriving at more advanced cognitive strategies than that verified in students working by themselves (Moro, 1987). Grouping students with homogeneous talents seems to be essential in order for them to achieve at the level of their abilities. On the other hand, motivation is always destabilized when new concepts are too easy or too difficult; challenge must be appropriate for the student's level of readiness (Feldhusen & Moon, 1992).

Evidence generated by research further supports the advantages of flexible group tasks, with substantial academic gain particularly in the case of gifted and talented students. Special grouping becomes even more necessary for students whose levels of achievement, attitudes, learning styles, and motivations are exceptionally high and whose educational needs far exceed the demands of the regular classroom.

The process of grouping must be flexible, with activities based largely on the curiosity, ability levels, and learning styles of the students themselves. A sensible practice is to link student needs directly to program activities and then appraise their progress periodically. Some students work at a fast pace and deal well with more complex material; grouping these students together is important for them to work at their full potential. Appropriate group practice will give all students equal opportunities to participate in different and advanced classes, with the objective of meeting their individual learning needs.

The concept of giftedness and theories about intelligence have transformed over the past decade. Educators have become more aware of the need for individuals with greater talent and gifts to receive special mentoring and support. As a consequence, the field of education and society itself need to create the conditions and means to facilitate learning for gifted individuals.

One of the current underlying premises of many educational programs is that, regardless of aptitude and talent, individuals rarely achieve a level of excellence without adequate stimulation and advising. When special programs are not available, the only alternative for gifted and talented students is conventional education. Lack of special assistance may lead to the waste of their aptitudes and talents, as well as loss of motivation.

Assuming that the gifted student has the same rights as anyone else to be educated at the level of his or her talents, aptitudes, and abilities, several important facts regarding the educational needs of the gifted have been considered in the reviewed bibliography (Sabatella, 1995):

- They thrive both on formal and nonformal education.
- They reach their greatest achievement in stimulating environments that favor the development and expansion of their abilities and the broadening of their interests.
- They need creative experience, artistic, scientific, and technological support, and recreation and sports with other gifted children. They also need stimulating programs that allow student participation in research projects, field trips, visits, camps, and community projects or events.
- Because they possess a wide range of interests and abilities, they also need special educational programs to accommodate individual objectives.
- They need to find challenge focusing on important and useful ideas to broaden creative, academic, and personal horizons; project greater objectives; and develop a sense of responsibility and intellectual independence.
- They must not be withdrawn from the world where they live, for they must learn how to cope with the differences between their personal potential and that of others.
- They need to know about dynamic learning methods that are compatible with their greater speed of reasoning and their exceptional cognitive ability.

To create enough challenge, educators must focus on the development of gifted students' entire personality and abilities. This goal cannot be achieved if attention is paid only to the enrichment and broadening of a single talent area.

Although information satisfies the student's deep natural drive to learn, information is not enough:

Educating a child is not simply to offer something that will be added to his or her life, conscience, and personality. It is to inspire, to awaken and to motivate the power which he or she already has; it is to help him or her to achieve interior growth and, as a consequence, to express himself or herself to the exterior world. (Ordem Rosacruz—AMORC, 1989, p. 9)

When the emotional and educational needs are not met, very intelligent people may become socially disastrous. Curricula for the gifted, therefore, must include formal opportunities for the students to learn to reflect on their own values as well as the values of others (Baska, 1985).

The program must bring into focus their emotional and social needs and their practical application in adult life; students must be empowered to cope with situations of failure and frustration, and they must understand the concepts of challenge and loss without fear. They should know they have the right to make mistakes and that problem solving is not just useful for school tests but also for life. Because gifted people generally act as leaders in their groups and will naturally be leaders in the future, morality, justice, ethics, and responsibility also emerge as absolutely necessary dimensions of study.

## THE RELATIONSHIP WITH THE COMMUNITY

Children's talents should be nurtured as early as possible so that they can achieve their full potential. The interaction and commitment between schools, families, and community enable outstanding students to extend their study and develop their potential at a pace and depth that match their abilities.

Active participation in the community and the use of its resources are necessary for special programs to achieve service excellence. Many resources outside schools may be used to extend educational opportunities for both gifted and regular classroom students. By paying attention to what the children like to do (e.g., a hobby such as drawing or working with numbers), parents and teachers can help them explore resources and develop their interests and talents. They can take children to places that offer hands-on activities and expose them to new fields and subjects. They can involve the children in story times at the library or bookstores and special events at museums and community centers.

The most effective community resources for educational programs are found at obvious places. One needs to look carefully, however, for those community organizations and institutes that would work most effectively with gifted students. Materials and equipment may be obtained at universities, research centers, museums, libraries, laboratories, galleries, art institutes, radio and TV studios, industries, and other institutions. Events, artistic shows, science fairs and exhibits also offer invaluable resources for learning enrichment (Sabatella, 1995).

Educators should involve institutions, commerce, and industry much more in their teaching. They can network with community resources to place gifted students in trainee or apprenticeship situations, as well as in mentoring relationships with professional leaders. These resources generally come from established groups that generate a large number of educational opportunities. The community may offer not only materials and equipment but also the invaluable expertise of specialists, scientists, artists and musicians, craftspersons, technicians, researchers, and leaders. These professionals and other creative and productive people may act as tutors, teachers, and role models for students with special talents.

As educators, we constantly need to optimize learning opportunities, creating links between the school, the family, and the community. We must offer our most gifted students an experience that allows for the broadening of their interests and for the development of their exceptional abilities.

## CONCLUSION

Teachers, parents, support staff, and tutors play a critical role in the lives of gifted children. They are facilitators for the total development of their talents and the realization of their dreams and hopes. Because of the vital importance of these facilitators, we must continue preparing them and increasing their number to meet the needs of more gifted students (Seeley, 1985).

Talent does not choose social class, sex, race, or nationality. Giftedness and talent are present in all cultural groups, across all economic strata, and in all areas of human endeavor. As educators, we should try to understand gifted students in all their variety, recognize their talents, guide their activities, foster their interests, stimulate their participation in society, and create an adequate environment for their development.

Rather than reflecting on a George Gershwin of the past, it seems plausible to reflect on the millions of Georges whom we could not reach because their potential was lost. Rather than recalling Fernando Pessoa, Frida Kahlo, Albert Sabin, Mohandas Gandhi, Marie Curie, and Martin Luther King Jr., who managed to live up to their potential, let us reach out to the millions of Fernandos, Alberts, Mohandas, and Martins who are right now looking for the support, interest, and the enthusiasm of someone who can help them achieve the greatest artistic, literary, scientific, social, political, or technological height, thus advancing world progress.

# 11

## *The Role of Summer Programs*

### *Providing Support for Students, Parents, and Schools*

*Pam Piskurich*

Traditionally, summer school has signified failure of a class or the need for remedial work. It was a time to "make up" what was missed during the course of the regular school year, often viewed by children and their peers as a punishment for not performing well in school. This is not the case for summer programs and camps for the talented and creative student. Talented students need challenging materials presented at a fast pace that provide them with the opportunity to develop a thorough background in their subject and allow them to progress to more advanced material when they are ready (Lupkowski & Assouline, 1992).

Summer programs for gifted and talented students generally provide content-concentrated lessons that encourage students to discover and tackle educational challenges as they develop and grow academically. This chapter will discuss the role of summer programs, the benefits of participation, identification of students for summer programs, and a sample program.

## THE ROLE OF SUMMER PROGRAMS

What do summer programs offer for talented youth? "Summer programs provide a level of challenge and a pace of learning that is more suitable to the intellectual capabilities of gifted students and very different from what they encounter in school" (Oszewski-Kubilius, 1997, p. 180). Many summer programs for the gifted are sponsored by institutions of higher education and vary in many ways. There are programs that offer a wide range of content and course possibilities. Some offer accelerated courses that students take to earn college credit; others give students the opportunity to investigate nontraditional topics.

Although some summer programs prefer giving students a sample of several different areas of study, others allow students to concentrate on a single subject area. Most enable students to delve further into topics of special interest to them or branch out into new areas. Special programs for talented children may be necessary to "rescue" them from a pattern of underachievement that can result from spending too much time in "easy" or "boring" classes (Rimm, 1991).

In addition to providing an excellent academic experience, summer programs for gifted students also offer opportunities for social development. Classes with other gifted children are more likely to foster friendships based on common interests and priorities and social support for educational pursuits and talent development (Oszewski-Kubilius, Grant, & Seibert, 1993). This may be the first time in their academic lives that the students are grouped with similar-ability peers.

One such example of grouping students homogeneously is the C-MITES (Carnegie Mellon Institute for Talented Elementary Students) Summer Program. C-MITES offers a summer camp for talented third through seventh graders at sites throughout the state of Pennsylvania. The program provides students with a hands-on approach to the sciences, mathematics, and humanities. The students participate in a variety of activities to enhance their learning and are actively involved in their courses. The program aims to bring together talented elementary students in an academically challenging and stimulating situation (C-MITES, 2001).

The success of the students in a summer program involves erasing the traditional views and opinions that accompany the notion of summer schooling. Academic stimulation and desire to discover make the summer-time experience extremely rewarding. Grouping gifted students who have similar interests and are working toward a common goal in a challenging atmosphere is a rewarding experience for all involved.

## WHO ARE THE STUDENTS?

Who are the students that qualify for a summer program? Most programs offer guidelines for acceptance, tuition requirements, age restrictions, and other basic requirements for participation. Some programs require students to be in a gifted program at their regular school or participate in a talent search. Other programs require parent observation checklists. Students selected for summer programs enjoy learning and actively seek opportunities for intellectual challenge and enrichment. These students perform well academically, display creativity, and have good work habits. Most of the applications for gifted programs require standardized achievement test scores, teacher recommendation forms, report cards, and information about the students' social activities such as hobbies and club memberships.

The C-MITES summer program criteria are presented here as an example of some typical application requirements for a summer camp for talented and gifted youth. Students begin the application for the C-MITES summer program by participating in the Elementary Student Talent Search. Students eligible for the talent search must be in third through sixth grades. They must have scored in the 95th percentile or above on at least one section of a nationally averaged standardized test such as the Iowa Tests of Basic Skills, Stanford Achievement Test, or the California Achievement Test. These talented students are then invited to take an above-level test called the "EXPLORE" (which was developed by the American College Testing Program). The EXPLORE test is an eighth-grade test that is administered to younger children. The test helps determine the areas of strength as well as weakness for the individual student. It is also used as a guide for acceptance into the C-MITES summer program. Recommended EXPLORE scores are given for each of the summer classes offered.

The talent search is open to students who may not be in their school's gifted program; they may qualify for the search based on one individual score from the qualifying test submitted. The talent search helps to identify those students who are particularly talented in a specific area (for further information regarding talent searches, see Assouline & Lupkowski-Shoplik, 1997). The child then receives an invitation to take a course in the subject area where he or she demonstrates exceptional ability. This can be very beneficial for the student's self-esteem and self-worth. If the child seems unchallenged in a particular content area and perhaps average in overall class ranking, a summer program in this area may be appropriate. Students should pursue a class in the subjects in which they excel as well as in areas that interest them. After testing, the students must then complete a summer program application.

The C-MITES summer program application provides lists of the summer schedule, including dates, times, locations, and courses available in a particular geographic area. The application has demographic questions as well as questions about the children's hobbies, interests, and current school situation. Parents also answer questions about their talented child. The students provide a copy of their test scores, report card, and a recommendation from their teacher in their regular school. Students who perform well on the EXPLORE, have strong teacher recommendations, and have good grades may then participate in the C-MITES summer program offered at a local school, university, or college. C-MITES uses a rigorous application process that provides the most talented and creative students the opportunity to participate together. The successful completion of all requirements for acceptance into the program serves as a predictor of the potential challenge and success of the student in a particular course.

When applying to a summer program, the applicants should provide all of the necessary information to avoid delay and ensure the child's participation. The applicants should carefully read all the requirements and inquire about financial obligations as well as scholarships and aid awarded to those who demonstrate financial need.

## WHAT ARE THE ACTIVITIES?

By design, activities for the C-MITES summer program are mostly hands-on and challenging. The students design experiments, test their own hypotheses, and present their findings. The programs encourage students to be active participants. The activities require time to complete and, because of the amount of time involved, may not be a part of the child's regular curriculum. Often, the activities used in the C-MITES courses are mentioned in the structure of a regular classroom for students to explore on their own or complete outside of class for additional enrichment.

The C-MITES summer program is offered in many areas throughout the state of Pennsylvania. The classes are typically offered for 1 or 2 weeks and take place from 9 a.m. until noon, daily. C-MITES students may participate in optional extended day activities after the morning program. The courses complement what students have studied in school and provide them with challenges in mathematics, science, or humanities. They are designed to be stimulating and fun academic experiences. Students engage in advanced content at a level and pace appropriate for gifted children. For example, in mathematics classes, students use manipulatives to study mathematics topics that are typically reserved for older students. In one of the science classes, students go on a simulated archaeological dig and reconstruct the skeleton found inside a regurgitated owl pellet. The classes stress problem solving, investigating patterns and relationships, and "doing" mathematics, science, and humanities rather than simply learning algorithms or memorizing formulas. Picture the student measuring the velocity of a roller coaster and understanding principles of centrifugal and centripetal forces. Students actually do just that in one of the popular summer courses called amusement park physics. In this course, the students explore, measure, and experience speed, acceleration, G-forces, weightlessness, motion, and gravity. An elevator and a playground serve as "simulators" as they prepare for the culminating activity, going to an amusement park and testing their conjectures. Students go on exciting rides and record data to experience physics!

Another popular C-MITES course is robotics. In this course, the students build robots and program them to perform tasks. They plan and design a robotic arm and then program that arm to lift and transport objects from one spot to another. They learn how to program a robot to cruise the perimeter of a tabletop without falling off. They design a robot capable of ascending an inclined plane and defending itself against another robot in a wrestling match. Students design the robot and then build their designs. They test their robots and redesign them much like real roboticists do. Activities emphasize the development of students' capabilities in making and using robots suitable for a variety of manufacturing processes. Student participants also visit Carnegie Mellon's Robotics institute and talk with practicing roboticists.

Another course, called "Blast Off," provides students with the opportunity to discover the principles of flight. The students fly kites and paper airplanes to understand the aerodynamic principles of flight. They record the experimental data on the computer and create graphs to explain their discoveries to their parents on parent visitation day. They design, construct, and fly their own hot air balloon created with their choice of materials. They study rocketry and launch rockets, measuring distance traveled and altitude. Other experiments are performed to investigate Bernoulli's principle and Newton's laws by using everyday material such as balloons, pop bottles, and water. They make many discoveries during their 2-week space mission exploring aeronautics and space travel.

These are just a few of the activities and courses offered in the C-MITES summer program. Other topics of interest to the students include probability, statistics, geometry, applied mathematics, physics, chemistry, electronics, lasers, magnetism, computer programming, journalism, and writing. Students are placed in groups based on their age, interest, grades, and scores on the EXPLORE test. Class size is limited to 20 students, with one instructor and one teaching assistant. Students participate in small-group, individual, and whole-class activities. The National Council of Teachers of Mathematics, the National Science Teachers Association, and the National Council of Teachers of English have recommended a number of the activities incorporated into the C-MITES summer program. The national standards of education are also used in planning and designing the summer program courses.

## WHY PARTICIPATE? WHAT ARE THE BENEFITS?

Organizers of special programs believe that participation in summer programs is highly beneficial to gifted and talented students (Oszewski-Kubilius, 1997). Research completed on summer programs suggests the following benefits:

- positive feelings due to involvement in a learning situation that presents a more appropriate match between the students' intellectual abilities and the challenge or rigor of a course;
- growth in acceptance of others, knowledge of different cultures, and enhanced worldview as a result of participating with a more diverse group of students; and
- self-testing of abilities due to placement in an intellectually challenging situation and subsequent reevaluations and goal setting that can further a student's progress in attaining excellence (Oszewski-Kubilius, 1997, pp. 182-183).

A rigorous summer program that exposes students to challenging material at a fast pace provides the academic stimulation they need and rarely get in the regular classroom. They also enjoy the hands-on approach to learning, appreciate their teachers' enthusiasm, and like socializing with other students. C-MITES is a good example of a program that enables students to create their own ideas and explore various ways of testing, experimenting with, and expressing them. Because the courses are hands-on, students become actively engaged in a learning process that is consistently fast-paced, fun, and stimulating.

Enersen (1993) studied the benefits of summer programs for gifted students. When the summer program participants of her research were interviewed, they stated that the summer programs provided the following:

- Academic challenge
- Appropriate peer relationships
- Improved self-understanding and self-confidence

Summer programs may also support family relationships. Parents find it helpful to support their children in preparing for the daily activities and challenges they encounter. The experiences that the children share with their families are often high-energy and motivational conversations. A student who academically "rambles on" about what he or she did in class today and what he or she is going to do tomorrow is a joy for all parents to hear.

## WHO ARE THE TEACHERS?

Instructors in the C-MITES summer program are certified teachers who have strong backgrounds in the content areas they teach. They are selected because of their excellent teaching skills, mastery of the subject, enthusiasm, and interest in working with young children. Most of the teachers are secondary certified in a specific discipline. Some of the summer program instructors are university instructors and professionals. Regardless of their background, all of them enjoy teaching gifted children and nurturing the development of their strengths and talents.

The true strength of any program is in the planning and enthusiasm of its instructional staff. The teachers design lessons that focus on problem solving (rather than memorization) and that foster discovery through experimentation. The teachers guide the students on their quest and journey into the unknown. The only "drill" in the classroom can be heard when "plugged in" to the wall. The faculty is carefully chosen from public schools, private schools, and universities. In addition to their demonstrated excellence in their fields, they share a common bond and commitment to educating talented youngsters.

# SUPPORTING THE SCHOOLS

Because the teachers come from the local community, there is a natural connection between the summer curriculum and what the students cover in a regular school year. The instructors are familiar with what the children learn throughout the school year, and consequently, they can design the summer program courses to supplement that curriculum. The material is designed to enhance and challenge the students in ways they rarely experience.

The program creates advanced content that not only stretches the students' abilities but relates this content to the instruction they receive in the local schools. This type of supportive relationship expands the child's view of education and learning. The schools provide the initial test scores and make recommendations for the students who may benefit from a challenging program. This ensures a rigor in summer programs for gifted students.

# FINDING A PROGRAM

Because gifted students by definition are in a minority, it is necessary to have vocal and visible support groups within the community (Davis & Rimm, 1989). Families can find summer programs in their area by contacting nearby colleges, universities, museums, schools, and the local library. They can check the local newspapers as well as church and community bulletin boards. The Internet can also be a valuable source of information on programs for the gifted.

Parents may also want to consider joining a local group such as PAGE (Pennsylvania Association for Gifted Education) or a national group such as NAGC (National Association for Gifted Children) to receive mailings and other information about summer programs in their particular area. A benefit of membership in such organizations is that parents make a clear statement to their children that education and challenge are valued in their family (Davis & Rimm, 1989). The school guidance counselor should have information regarding summer programs. Oftentimes, information is on file in the school's offices, and because staff personnel are not provided

**Table 11.1**  Checklist for Choosing a Summer Program

| Questions to Consider | Possible Responses |
|---|---|
| Type of program | Residential or commuter camps |
| Duration | 9 a.m. to noon or 9 a.m. to 5 p.m. |
| Academic interests | Science |
| Social interests | Boy/Girl Scouts |
| Daily organization of the program | Snack breaks/lunch breaks |
| Resources available | Computer room/planetarium |
| Staff | Certified teachers/college professors |
| Financial obligations | Aid available |
| Class size | Limited to 20 |
| Application | Deadline date |
| Evaluation | Well-known and established program |
| Individual goals | Child's interest in the summer program |

*Research Completed*
List the programs investigated and find the one that best matches the
    interests, abilities, and developmental need of the child.

with ample copies for the student body, they wait for parents to approach them about different programs.

Parents should select summer programs that will prepare their children for the year ahead and provide new material to help them explore their creative talents. Parents may wish to consider programs for strengthening skills, extending conceptual understanding, exploring creative strengths, and having fun with the learning process. When searching for programs for gifted youth, parents might prepare a checklist outlining the desires they have for the program. The student could also prepare one. Table 11.1 shows how such a checklist can help families match the interests, abilities, and developmental needs of the children to the opportunities available in summer programs.

Parents need to research thoroughly the programs available. They need to find one that best matches the needs of their children. Other children who have participated in the program can be helpful. Ask questions about class size, staff, locations, dates, and times. Choose between a commuter class and a residential program. An individual student may benefit from both types. Age is a factor in that decision, and there are benefits for each type. Residential programs are recommended for high school students; through exposure to a college or university campus, these students can prepare for their academic future. Decide the daily duration of the program.

Do you want the child involved in full-day or half-day activities? Also decide the program duration. Do you want a 1-, 2-, 3-, or 4-week program? A variety of programs offer all of these options.

In searching for a summer program, consider the activities involved. Students enjoy being outdoors during the summertime, and the outdoor classroom can be a great place to learn. Also compare the number of children in the class versus the number of teachers. Smaller groups can accommodate the individual needs of a student better than larger ones. Look for a program that has limits on class size. The smaller the class size, the more individualized and personal the learning will be. Find out the ratio of student to teacher before enrolling in a program. Most important, always discuss programming options with the children. If they feel eager and excited about the summer program, the experience will be rewarding for all involved. Encourage the children to choose topics that they do well and that interest them. Entering a program with an inquiring mind and a desire for discovery puts children on the right track. Finally, stress the importance of having fun.

So, now that school is out for the summer, is the opportunity to learn still an option? What are your plans for the summer? Will you travel? Will the children take courses? Will you explore new topics and interests with your children or send them to a special program? Will they go to a sports camp, an arts studio, a theater workshop, or a science lab? Will they surf the ocean or the Internet? Regardless of what you do, remember that the summertime, for your gifted children, offers a rare opportunity to learn freely—to explore, create, and innovate at a level they rarely can at any other time. In this regard, summer gifted programs can make the difference between long periods of boredom and the excitement so often expressed by children newly awakened to fields and ideas they never encountered before.

# 12

## Support for Gifted Programs

### Parents, School, and Community

*Deborah E. Bordelon*

*There are always two people in every picture: the photographer and the viewer.*

—Ansel Adams

Like a photographer's tripod, gifted programs are supported by three components: school, parents, and community. Each component of this triad provides an element of support that enables the gifted program to survive. In addition, each of these components has its own set of unique needs. To view this relationship as a tripod clarifies the relationship; each leg of the triad is necessary for stability. If one leg is removed, then stability is in jeopardy.

The purpose of this chapter is to examine the interacting roles of parents, schools, and communities in support and advocacy for gifted programs. All programs for the gifted, whether at the elementary or secondary level, need the support provided by these three components.

The suggestions provided are relevant to teachers of the gifted, school administrators, and university faculty involved in the development and implementation of gifted programs. Just as a photographer chooses a developing process to enhance the image captured on film, advocates of gifted education must examine appropriate avenues for increasing support for gifted programs. Program awareness and involvement of all stakeholders generate advocacy. The underlining premise is that without advocacy from all components of the triad, gifted programs do not survive. The interaction among the triad elements results in effective advocacy, and each element of the advocacy triad will be examined in light of its contribution to the complete picture of gifted education.

# ROLE OF THE SCHOOL

The first component of this triad is the school. The school's role is to provide effective programming for gifted centers that deliver appropriate and defensible instruction for their gifted students. *Defensible* may be defined as a program that meets the individual needs of the students, addresses differentiation from the general education curriculum in process and product, and is supported by research. Many researchers in the field have proposed programming structures that tap into all of these areas. Two programs that exemplify appropriate and defensible programming for gifted students are the integrated curriculum model and the enrichment triad model.

Van Tassel-Baska (1997) proposed the integrated curriculum model, which focuses on the interrelated areas of advanced content knowledge, higher order thinking and processing, and learning experiences that deal with major issues and themes in the context of both real-world applications and theoretical modeling within and across disciplines. Another model that clearly addresses the areas needed for a defensible gifted program is the enrichment triad model (Renzulli & Reis, 1985, 1997). The program described in the enrichment triad model consists of three levels of activities. Type I activities focus on general explorations that expose students to a wide variety of disciplines, topics, and ideas. Type II activities center on group training that enables students to develop problem-solving, critical thinking, oral, written, and visual communication skills. Type III activities involve the student in self-selection of topics and real-world investigations that employ the skills learned in Type II.

Differentiation is a key component of any gifted program. Tomlinson (1995) identified the components of an appropriately differentiated classroom. These components are as follows:

1. Concept-focused and principle-driven instruction

2. Built-in ongoing assessment of student readiness and growth

3. Flexible grouping based on the task or need

4. Active student learning facilitated by the teacher

The need for differentiated instruction is as great for the gifted child as it is for the child with other exceptionalities. The manner in which instruction is differentiated for students who are gifted often determines how defensible the program is.

Gifted education often provides services in small groups. Programming is based on the students' grade level, with everyone working on the same activity or skill. The need for individualized instruction, which has been the battle cry of special education for years, is just as necessary in this instance. Renzulli and Reis (1991) emphasized this point by stating that effective programming focuses on the development of behavioral potential and interest, not convenience or chronological age grouping. An essential component of any defensible gifted program, according to Tomlinson (1995), is a curriculum that differentiates in three main areas: content, process, and product. If the curriculum for the gifted program focuses on enrichment activities that keep the learning on a superficial level (such as using activities in isolation with little or no connection with a content area or discipline), the program may lose credibility. For gifted programs to benefit the target population, they need to assess how individualized, rigorous, and in-depth is the instruction.

Trained personnel are necessary to recognize strengths and weaknesses in the program and its curriculum. The school plays a major role in this area. Training teachers to provide differentiated instruction is a necessity. This training should encompass not only teachers within the gifted program but all teachers. Many of the students who participate in gifted programs will receive the majority of their instruction in the general classroom. It is a wise investment, therefore, for the teaching faculty of a school to be well trained in recognizing gifted behaviors and providing differentiated instruction in the classroom setting. This type of training can promote a sense of awareness and community at the school.

Teachers are more likely to collaborate when they have a common understanding about the direction and goals of the curriculum. Collaboration among the general education faculty and the teachers of the gifted improves not only professional relationships but also the education of all students in the school. Collaborative relationships need focus to be successful. Structuring discussions around relevant topics is beneficial to both parties. Recommendations from a National Association for Gifted Children task force focused on the following areas of discussion to improve communication among all educators: (a) expanding the understanding and perception of gifted education; (b) identifying effective instructional practices and programming; (c) preparing preservice, inservice, and graduate students for education of the gifted; (d) instituting policy and political action; (e) having school reform; and (f) conducting research and its dissemination (Tomlinson, Coleman, Allan, Udall, & Landrum, 1996).

Teachers often have close relationships with the parents of their students as well as with the community at large. If teachers have misperceptions of gifted children and the need for special programming, then these misperceptions often spread to the parents and community. As a result, community support of the program wanes. Teacher awareness and training cannot be stressed enough in providing a solid foundation for gifted programs.

# ROLE OF THE PARENTS

Parental involvement provides the second component of this triad supporting gifted programs. The parent has many roles within the school and community. Two roles are advocate and liaison to the community. One of the major roles for the parent of a student in the gifted program is as an advocate. The school needs to maintain strong ties with parents by sharing the program with them and involving them wherever possible. It is difficult for anyone to be an advocate for a program when there has not been adequate experience or sufficient knowledge of the program.

Parents naturally want to know what the school is doing to provide effective instruction for their children. An overview of the program, a description of the curriculum, and the types of activities that will be conducted during the school year can be effectively disseminated to parents at before-school meetings, afterschool meetings, or at socials. It may also be advantageous to do this twice a year—once in August and once in January—because some children enter the program after school has started, and their parents may not feel comfortable getting actively involved at midyear. These parent meetings are opportunities to tap into parents' areas of expertise as well as their ties to the community through business, social, and other contacts.

It is important that teachers and administration involve parents with the gifted program by inviting them to share their own knowledge about topics, help plan and organize field trips, or assist in the classroom. A school can easily find out what areas of expertise parents have by sending home questionnaires about interests, abilities, and avocations. Teachers can develop mini-courses and seminars from this information that would benefit and enrich all students. Through these activities, parents become more active members of the school community and play a more critical role in the development of curriculum and special programming.

Parents of gifted children may also request assistance from the school to create a support network for them in the gifted program. Information on how to enhance and expand children's abilities as well as how to obtain effective and low-cost enrichment materials for home use can be shared through meetings and workshops (Schwartz, 1997). This network could also provide identification and programming procedures to all parents. The establishment of a support network is especially important for parents from culturally diverse backgrounds who may not feel comfortable requesting information from the school in the traditional manner (Schwartz, 1997).

Parents are the liaisons between the school and community. Parental views of education are powerful influences on the community's perspective, and this is especially true when looking at programs for the gifted. When parents are knowledgeable about their child's program and aware of the importance of its continuation, they are much more likely to lobby for support of the school and gifted program.

## ROLE OF THE COMMUNITY

The community comprises the third leg in the triad. Too often, the links between the school and community are limited to fund-raising issues. Yet, a community has a wealth of resources—human, cultural, and professional—beyond the monetary. For example, when using authentic assessment in the classroom, local experts in the field may evaluate projects as well as provide feedback to the students, richly enhancing the experience. If the students are assigned to put together a photo essay of a chosen topic, it is logical to invite local photographers into the classroom to critique the projects based on their knowledge and expertise. This approach could be applied to any project undertaken in the classroom. A partnership with local writers, artists, architects, scientists, and entrepreneurs enables the students to encounter the standards and expectations within these fields. It allows the students' work to move beyond meeting the classroom requirements to meeting real-life standards. These partnerships also enable the members of the community to actively take part in the educational process—to become more fully engaged with students and the school system. Most important, it enhances the sense of community ownership in the school system.

The recruitment of people interested in participating in the assessment process involves contacting businesses by telephone or mail. Person-to-person contacts can also be very effective. These tactics allow for dialogue about the program and enable the teacher to share the goals, experiences, and projects of the program with community members.

Another way to involve the community is to develop a mentorship program. The pairing of a student with a mentor in the community provides that student an opportunity to explore a field of interest in much greater depth than can be provided in the classroom. The student gains firsthand experience of the daily workings of the mentor's profession and will be able to make wiser career decisions based on those experiences. At the secondary level, a mentor program may be established as part of the curriculum in which the student attends classes for part of the day and then works with the mentor the rest. Piirto (1999) suggested that a mentor fulfill four functions: (a) role model, (b) intellectual stimulation, (c) emotional support, and (d) professional network.

Mentoring may also be used at the elementary level. At this level, the students may not work with the mentor on a daily basis; however, a schedule may be devised in which the student can meet with a mentor regularly (e.g., biweekly or monthly) to address a special interest. Elementary students may also spend a day at a particular business or work setting as part of a field trip or invite the mentor to come to class to explain aspects of his or her profession. Career days also encourage community members to share their expertise.

As a result of the limited funding designated for gifted programs, it is often necessary to go outside of the school system to find funding. Community businesses may be viable sources of grants or in-kind donations of equipment or supplies. If a business provides funding or equipment, it is extremely important to inform the business how the program intends to use it. Sharing photographs of projects created with the donated materials or pictures of the students using the equipment enables the businesses to see how their investments are benefiting students. Student-developed Web pages may be another vehicle for sharing information on classroom projects. Business owners may be invited to the class to celebrate the completion of a project or to participate in a student's presentation, enhancing the link between school and community as well. The inclusion of articles in the school and local newspapers acknowledging the business' support, outlines of how the materials are used in the program, and descriptions of the resulting products can greatly enhance relations with the community. As stated by Renzulli and Reis (1991), documentation is the key to building advocacy. Gifted program supporters are more likely to continue support and encourage others to join the effort when they see tangible evidence of the impact of their contributions on student learning.

One example of a program that clearly and effectively incorporates all three elements of school, parents, and community is the schoolwide enrichment model (Renzulli & Reis, 1985). The links between the school's program and the community are strengthened through the involvement of parents and community members in Type I activities (general exploratory activities) such as guest speakers, field trips, and so on. Community members may also become involved in Type II (group training activities) and Type III (individual and small-group investigations of real problems) activities through mentoring students as they gain knowledge in a particular field and apply it to real-world situations. Because the schoolwide enrichment model uses a more inclusive procedure for having students participate in these activities, the advocacy base may easily expand to include not only the parents of students formally identified but also parents of all students who participate in and benefit from the enrichment experience (Renzulli & Reis, 1991).

Many exciting and stimulating activities occur in the school setting that the community may never hear about. Unfortunately, it is largely the negative aspects of education that make it to the newspaper, and the community forms opinions of the educational system based on that information. Teachers of the gifted are frequently required to not only teach their students but also engage in public relations campaigns at the school and community levels for the continuation of their programs. To have a program of substance is one of the best public relations tools available.

The dissemination of accurate information about the gifted program is often the responsibility of the teacher of the gifted. The targeted audiences for this information include other teachers at the school, administrators, parents, and community members. What goes on in the gifted program should never be shrouded in secrecy, hidden away from the rest of the school. This only encourages cries of elitism and promotes misperceptions of gifted students and the programs designed for them. These misperceptions often distort the picture of the gifted program. Collaboration among the three components of the triad (school, parents, and community) is critical to the development and growth of all students.

# 13

# *Assessment*

## *Impact on Children, Parents, and Teachers*

### *Cheryll M. Adams*

## ASSESSMENT ISSUES

The effects of traditional assessment maintain a somewhat biased educational system and reduce learning to survival of the fittest. Those who enter school already behind get further behind, receive poor grades, and have little chance of becoming successful under the current system of assessment. Students may also incorporate their grades into their self-concept and categorize themselves as "successes" or "failures."

Instead of thinking about assessment as a way to measure what kids do and do not know, try to think about assessment as a vehicle, a way of

Author's Note: Some of the research for this chapter was supported under the Javits Act Program (Grant No. R206R00001), as administered by the Office of Educational Research and Improvement, U.S. Department of Education. Grantees undertaking such projects are encouraged to express freely their professional judgment. This chapter, therefore, does not necessarily represent positions or policies of the government, and no official endorsement should be inferred.

knowing. Assessment is a way of knowing that can involve many different values and perspectives than are traditionally included in measurement. This is particularly important in an out-of-school program where formal assessments such as paper-and-pencil tests may not be required or necessary. We still need to know if the student gained in knowledge, skills, techniques, and problem-solving strategies; we need to know if the structure of the program, curriculum, and organization worked for all the stakeholders (students, counselors, teachers, parents, program planners); and we need to know if parents and members of the community recognized the value of our program.

## ASSESSING STUDENTS

### Guidelines for Selecting and Using Educational Assessments

When we assess students, we do so to gather information to use in educational decision making. Nitko (1996, pp. 5-6) provided the following guidelines for using educational assessment meaningfully.

1. Be clear about the learning target you want to assess.

2. Be sure that the assessment techniques you select actually match the learning target.

3. Be sure that the selected assessment techniques serve the needs of the learner.

4. Whenever possible, be sure to use multiple indicators of performance for each learning target.

5. Be sure that when you interpret the results of assessments, you take their limitations into account.

### Purposes of Assessment

*Understand Students in Their Contexts.*[1] One way of knowing students is to know them as individuals, know what they *can* do, identify their strengths, and see what you should do next. This information is ever changing. It eventually becomes obsolete as you see the child doing new and different things.

*Determine Students' Strengths and Weaknesses.* This is particularly important for minority and low socioeconomic (SES) children who may enter school already behind the majority of the other students, hiding their talents. By approaching assessment in this way, students have opportunities to allow their strengths to overshadow their weaknesses. In many cases, their strengths will provide you with new avenues to approach their weaknesses.

*Differentiate Instruction.* Using an unmodified curriculum with students whose abilities and strengths differ is inappropriate and imposes constraints on both teacher and students. Fitting the curriculum to the student, not vice versa, allows students freedom to learn in a welcoming environment and permits assessment to provide a truer picture of the child's abilities.

*Promote Students' Awareness of Their Learning* Individual conferences or interviews with children allow them to express their feelings about their strengths and weaknesses. Giving them some control over their assessment, such as, "When you think you are ready to show me your research design, let me know," allows students to proceed at their own pace and helps make them aware of their own progress.

*Document Students' Learning and Change.* To get a clear picture, we need alternative means of assessment other than traditional tests, quizzes, and assignments. Self-evaluation, teacher checklists, product and performance assessment, observation scales, teacher-student conferences, peer evaluation, and journaling are all ways that might be used to assess gifted students to determine their progress in your program. Several of these are discussed in the pages that follow. These alternate forms of assessment lend themselves quite well to minority or low SES children who may not perform well on traditional forms of assessment. These students often have different learning styles, thinking styles, and behavioral styles that are not tapped by traditional instruments. If you gather information in a variety of ways and piece all these things together, you can document how the child has learned and what you know about the child over time. The end result is not a way to compare children with each other but to see a child's progress through interaction with the learning environment.

*Communicate With Others Connected With Students (parents, teachers, principal, etc.).* Communication can be verbal, written, or interactive. Rating scales, checklists, narratives, personal notes, or interactive journals between teacher and parents are ways to let others know about the child's progress in terms of strengths and weaknesses.

## Assessing Gifted Students

In the regular classroom, teachers must deal with several issues when they assess gifted students. The typical end-of-chapter test may not tap into the wealth of knowledge that the gifted child has assimilated about a particular topic. Often, the classroom expectations do not take into account that the gifted child soaks up much more information than expected and can analyze, synthesize, and evaluate that information and apply it to new situations. Teachers who wish to develop more nontraditional measures are often hampered by state, district, and local constraints. Although the issues of assessment in regular classrooms are beyond the scope of this chapter, I mention the issue in contrast to what must occur in special programs for gifted students.

In out-of-school programs developed specifically for gifted and talented students, there is an assumption that assessment will be designed to address the expectations of these special classes. Generally, traditional paper-and-pencil tests provide too narrow a scope for assessing where the student is and where he or she needs to progress to reach full potential. The next section provides an annotated list of possible assessment tools that can be used to provide useful information about learner outcomes.

### Ways to Assess Students

*Peer Evaluation.* Students share their work with each other, in pairs, small groups, or the whole group. Students should have opportunities to develop the means of assessment along with the teacher. The evaluation instrument could be a checklist or answers to open-ended questions. Students could exchange papers and work in a peer-editing situation or give constructive comments about each other's work. You will have to work with students concerning appropriate ways to give feedback before using this method of evaluation.

*Self-Evaluation.* Again, have students assist in developing the assessment instrument. As with peer evaluation, questions may be asked in a variety of formats. Some examples are as follows: "I am pleased with the way my (project, book report, model, concept map, etc.) turned out," "I thought of other ideas while working on this one," and "I learned something new while working on this project." As with peer evaluations, students need to help set guidelines about the appropriate use of self-evaluation. "My work was good" doesn't carry much information.

*Teacher Evaluation.* Traditional paper-and-pencil tests, quizzes, questioning strategies aimed at higher level thinking, and working individually with a student are all forms of teacher evaluation.

*Product Assessment.* This type of assessment is usually a rating scale or a series of open-ended questions. The scale may be filled out by teachers, parents, the child, or another designated person. Some focus questions might be the following: To what extent does the product indicate close attention to detail? To what extent is this product beyond what a student of this age would be expected to produce?

*Portfolio.* Portfolios are ideal ways to view a child's work over a period of time. Both students and teachers, together or separately, choose work samples to place into the portfolio. Both should have input concerning the criteria for selecting a piece for the portfolio. The portfolio may be divided into several compartments, either by subject (math, language arts, etc.), by type of sample (reports, journals, quizzes, self-assessments, etc.), or by other methods. The purpose of the portfolio is multifaceted. In addition to showing growth (or lack thereof) over time, it helps develop a sense of process and serves as a way to empower both teacher and students. For example, a student selects a completed activity to add to the portfolio. The teacher and student sit down together and conference over the work in the portfolio. Both can construct information and inferences about the student's learning. Both can determine strengths and weaknesses in the subject and use that information as a guide for further learning.

*Evaluation by an Appropriate Audience.* Students should be encouraged to pursue "real-world" problems. It follows that these projects need to be evaluated by an appropriate audience. For example, a classification key to the trees in the city park could be presented to and evaluated by the local garden club. A work of art might be judged by local artists according to their standards.

*Pretests and Posttests (Yes, even in special programs!).* Pretests should be given at the beginning of a new section of study to determine who already knows some or all of the information. Posttests provide information about what was learned and what gaps still remain.

*Rating Scales.* Rating scales can be used for peer evaluation, self-evaluation, product assessment, and other types of assessment. Statements are listed, and the respondent indicates the extent of agreement with the statements. The scale may be of any length but is usually 3, 4, 5, or 10 units. For example, a 3-unit scale may be *agree, neutral,* and *disagree.* A 5-unit one may be *strongly agree, agree, neutral. disagree,* and *strongly disagree.* Other scales may look like this:

1    2    3    4    5    6    7    8    9    10

*strongly disagree*                                                 *strongly agree*

You could even use the "fist-to-five" technique by having the students indicate with their hands—fist being the most negative and five fingers being the most positive response.

*Teacher-Student and/or Student-Student Conferences.* Conferences allow both parties to engage in a dialogue about a particular work or assignment. For example, a teacher-student writing conference may involve the student explaining why she or he chose the topic, why a particular choice of words was used, and any personal meaning that may not be apparent.

*Appropriate Standardized Instruments.* Standardized instruments used to assess students must be appropriate to the construct being assessed. For example, the Torrance Test of Creative Thinking is not appropriate to assess general intelligence. When using an achievement test to assess content knowledge, be sure the test objectives match the objectives in your own curriculum. When assessing minority students, check to see if the test has been normed on that population and is not biased against these students.

*Journals.* Journal entries are usually not as structured as other response-type schoolwork. Journals may be used as a dialogue between teacher and student on any topic. Students have the opportunity to express their own ideas and opinions. At the same time, you can gain valuable insight into the student's writing abilities and thought processes.

*Observation Scales.* These may be scales or checklists and are ways for you to note particular target behaviors. For example, you may develop a checklist of group skills to use as you move around to each group in your classroom. You may want to check for cooperation, collaboration, interdependence, accountability, honoring others' opinions, and so on.

*Performance Assessment.* A performance assessment is used to see if students can apply, analyze, synthesize, and/or evaluate bits of curriculum that you have covered. Specific criteria (rubrics) are developed to score the task. For example, you want to assess the student's ability to interpret data. Students gather data from classmates by asking them a question such as, "What is your favorite candy?" They then tally the results. As part of the criteria for successfully completing the task, you might look to see if the student can (a) organize data into graph, table, or chart form; (b) read and interpret data presented in chart, table, or graph form; (c) analyze the data; and (d) make inferences based on the information available.

Parents should have a clear idea beforehand about the design of the program, a brief overview of the individual class their child has chosen so they know what you're doing (goals, content, processes, products, etc.), and what kind of feedback will be provided. A sample rating scale used by a teacher in a summer enrichment program is shown in Forms 13.1 and 13.2 . The scale was used to provide feedback to the parents and school personnel regarding the child's participation in the class.

## ASSESSING THE TEACHER AND OTHER ADULTS

As in regular school programs, teachers are evaluated periodically in special programs to assess their ability to provide meaningful learning experiences for gifted learners. Counselors, aides, intern teachers, and any other personnel who provide vital functions in the program must also be

**Form 13.1**  A Sample Evaluation Form from a Summer Enrichment Program

(This form would be filled out by the teacher as a summative assessment of the student during the program.)

| | *Frequently* | *Usually* | *Sometime* | *Seldom* |
|---|---|---|---|---|
| Demonstrates an application of concepts presented | | | | |
| Demonstrates risk-taking abilities | | | | |
| Expresses thoughts and feelings | | | | |
| Works cooperatively in a group | | | | |
| Works well independently | | | | |
| Demonstrates critical thinking skills | | | | |
| Uses science process skills | | | | |
| Uses problem-solving techniques | | | | |
| Participates in discussions | | | | |

**Form 13.2**  Checklist for Planning a Science Experiment

(This could be used as a self-assessment by the student before submitting the design to the teacher or as a teacher assessment of the design for a science investigation.)

| Criteria | Complete | Incomplete |
|---|---|---|
| States problem or question | | |
| States hypothesis | | |
| Arranges steps in sequential order | | |
| Lists materials needed | | |
| Defines terms used | | |
| Plans to observe | | |
| Plans to measure | | |
| Plans for data collection | | |
| States plan for interpreting data | | |
| States plan for making conclusion based on data | | |
| Indicates variables and control | | |

SOURCE: Adapted from Fowler (1990).

evaluated. These evaluations are generally multifaceted, allowing input from students, parents, program directors, and the teachers, counselors, aides, and interns themselves. Many of the forms of assessment discussed in relation to student assessment are also appropriate to use with this group. In addition to narratives resulting from classroom observation, checklists, and/or rating scales, reflective journaling and professional port-folios are also appropriate as self-evaluations for the personnel providing direct services to the children.

The National Association for Gifted Children (NAGC, 1994) has issued a position paper identifying competencies needed by teachers of gifted and talented students:

1. a knowledge and valuing of the origins and nature of high levels of intelligence, including creative expressions of intelligence;

2. a knowledge and understanding of the cognitive, social, and emotional characteristics, needs, and potential problems experienced by gifted and talented students from diverse populations;

3. a knowledge of and access to advanced content and ideas;

4. an ability to develop a differentiated curriculum appropriate to meeting the unique intellectual and emotional needs and interests of gifted and talented students; and

5. an ability to create an environment in which gifted and talented students can feel challenged and safe to explore and express their uniqueness.

Moon, Callahan, and Tomlinson (1999) found that teachers without special training in gifted education were not as effective at meeting the specific academic needs of gifted students as those who had special train-ing. In addition, a minimum standard under Guiding Principle Two of the Gifted Education Programming Criterion: Professional Development states, "Any teacher whose primary responsibility for teaching includes gifted learners must have extensive expertise in gifted education" (Landrum, Callahan, & Shaklee, 2001, p. 72). It would follow that evalua-tions of teachers of the gifted would attend to these competencies. Although there are several good teacher checklists and rating scales found in the literature, Form 13.3 was one created specifically for the evaluation of teachers in a 4-week summer workshop.

Many summer workshops have a residential component. Counselors in the program must also be trained to meet the social and emotional needs of these students because they stand in loco parentis for much of the nonacademic time. Form 13.4 is for evaluating counselors in a 1-week res-idential program for gifted students.

**Form 13.3**  Summer Workshop Teacher Evaluation

(This form could be modified to include a comment section under each
characteristic.)

Directions: Indicate the frequency at which the instructor exhibits the following
characteristics.

| Characteristic | Frequently | Sometimes | Rarely |
|---|---|---|---|
| Demonstrates understanding of gifted students | | | |
| Encourages risk taking | | | |
| Encourages higher level thinking skills | | | |
| Encourages creative thinking | | | |
| Designs effectively differentiated curriculum | | | |
| Encourages student ideas | | | |
| Conducts group discussions well | | | |
| Effectively uses a variety of teaching strategies | | | |
| Attends to students' social/ emotional needs | | | |

**Form 13.4**  Student Evaluation of Summer Residential Mathematics Program

Directions: For this part of the questionnaire, we would like you to consider the counselors and the activities you did outside your classes.

Circle the number that most closely matches your opinion. Use the following code:

| 1 = strongly disagree | 2 = disagree | 3 = undecided | 4 = agree | 5 = strongly agree |
|---|---|---|---|---|

| | | | | | |
|---|---|---|---|---|---|
| 1. The counselors got us involved in all activities. | 1 | 2 | 3 | 4 | 5 |
| 2. The counselors were enthusiastic and fun. | 1 | 2 | 3 | 4 | 5 |
| 3. I could count on the counselors to take care of something that might have been bothering me. | 1 | 2 | 3 | 4 | 5 |
| 4. I could trust the counselors. | 1 | 2 | 3 | 4 | 5 |
| 5. I would go to the counselors if I needed to talk and felt like he or she would listen. | 1 | 2 | 3 | 4 | 5 |
| 6. The counselors treated everyone with respect. | 1 | 2 | 3 | 4 | 5 |
| 7. The counselors listened to my opinion. | 1 | 2 | 3 | 4 | 5 |
| 8. The counselors disciplined us fairly. | 1 | 2 | 3 | 4 | 5 |

Other comments or suggestions:

## ASSESSING THE PROGRAM

Assessing the students and the teachers is often the main focus in both in-school and out-of-school program evaluations. What is often omitted, however, is an in-depth assessment of the impact of the program, in favor of what I call the .05 level of "I liked it." That is, students, parents, and other stakeholders are given lengthy questionnaires, the answers to which can be condensed to "Did you like 'it' or not?"

Coleman and Cross (2001) stated that programs for the gifted are difficult to evaluate because they *are* programs for the gifted. They described several difficulties: discovering a lack of agreement about what constitutes a gifted program, finding a comparison group, measuring program goals that deal with understanding abstract intellectual concepts and generation of novel thoughts, and constructing instruments to measure these. Callahan (2001) listed five areas that may be assessed when evaluating gifted programs: learner outcomes, cognitive outcomes, affective outcomes, individual outcomes, and group outcomes. Using the work of Coleman and Cross (2001) and Callahan (2001) as a guide, if we truly want to assess the impact of the program, then we first must be sure we can describe what we are going to evaluate! Program goals and objectives must be clearly articulated. Landrum et al. (2001) have edited an annotation to the NAGC program goals. This work is essential to anyone developing or evaluating a gifted program.

We have to figure out how we will define *success,* remembering that outcomes must be observable and measurable. The outcomes we are observing and measuring may be related to any of the stakeholders—parents, students, program planners, counselors, aides, administrators, community leaders, and other participants. In addition, data should be gathered from multiple sources, including but not limited to interviews, focus groups, standardized instruments, pretest and posttest scores, observations, and journals. The information gathered will be used to determine what is and isn't working; provide opportunities to discern how various stakeholders interpret the same questions, noting consistencies and inconsistencies; and identify areas that need fine-tuning or complete overhauls. The Callahan and Caldwell (1999) text on program evaluation is an invaluable guide to evaluating gifted programs. Chapter 5, which deals with evaluation concerns and questions, and Chapter 7, which discusses instrumentation, including instrument construction, are particularly helpful.

Form 13.5 presents a sample of a rating scale to gather data from the students concerning their response to the curriculum that was presented for the duration of the program. The statements were keyed to the teacher's goals and objectives, and the feedback helped her modify her curriculum to make a better match with her intended outcomes before she taught a new group of students. Similar questions could be asked to determine how students related to their counselors or other program personnel.

(text continued on p. 163)

**Form 13.5**  A Sample Student Evaluation Form for a Science Class

(This form would be filled out by the student to provide feedback to the teacher and program planner.)

Think about the class you attended during this session. Circle the number that most closely matches your opinion using the following code:

1 = strongly disagree    2 = disagree    3 = undecided    4 = agree    5 = strongly agree

| | | | | | |
|---|---|---|---|---|---|
| 1. I had the opportunity to learn about things that I do not ordinarily study at home. | 1 | 2 | 3 | 4 | 5 |
| 2. I learned science process skills such as observing, hypothesizing, gathering data, and drawing conclusions. | 1 | 2 | 3 | 4 | 5 |
| 3. I had the opportunity to use critical thinking skills to solve problems. | 1 | 2 | 3 | 4 | 5 |
| 4. I had the opportunity to work as a scientist would "in the real world." | 1 | 2 | 3 | 4 | 5 |
| 5. I felt challenged by the activities offered. | 1 | 2 | 3 | 4 | 5 |
| 6. My class was interesting. | 1 | 2 | 3 | 4 | 5 |
| 7. I enjoyed the learning experiences that I had in my class. | 1 | 2 | 3 | 4 | 5 |
| 8. What three activities did you enjoy the most? | _____ | | | | |
| 9. What would you change about this class to make it better? | _____ | | | | |

**Form 13.6** Teacher Evaluation of University Workshops for Gifted Youth

We are collecting data to determine whether these programs have been effective in helping students reach their potential. Please answer the following questions and write your comments or suggestions on this survey to help us better evaluate our programs.

The information gathered from this survey will be analyzed by an outside evaluator and reported to teachers, parents, administrators, and school board members. You may or may not include your name, and all information will remain confidential. Throughout the survey, the University Workshops for Gifted Youth will be referred to as the "Workshop Program."

Comments:

1. Rate the effectiveness of the Workshop Program.

   Good program          I don't know anything    Not a good program
                         about the program

2. To what extent do you feel the present identification process is effective in selecting the appropriate students for the Workshop Program?

   Effective process     I don't know what        Not a good process
                         the process is

3. To what extent do you feel the Workshop Program students show respect for others?

   Respect is shown      I haven't                Respect is lacking
                         observed this

4. To what extent do you feel students not involved in the Workshop Program or honors classes show respect for others?

   Respect is shown      I haven't                Respect is lacking
                         observed this

5. To what extent do you perceive the Workshop Program students as leaders?

   Leadership is         I haven't                Leadership is lacking
   demonstrated          observed this

6. To what extent do you feel regular class students perceive each other as leaders?

Leadership is        I haven't        Leadership is
demonstrated         observed this    lacking

7. To what extent are you currently differentiating the curriculum and instructional strategies for the range of students that you have in your classroom?

I plan a variety of lessons  I try to plan some   I don't have time to
in each curriculum area      variation in         plan different lessons
                             instructional strategies

List an example of differentiation:

8. What do you feel are the most positive aspects of the Workshop Program?

9. How would you change the Workshop Program?

If there are other comments you would like to make, use another piece of paper to attach to the survey. Thank you for your time and consideration.

---

**Form 13.7**  Student Evaluation of University Workshops for Gifted Youth

Please rate the following items using the scale provided below.

1. Have you had the opportunity to select topics and projects of interest to you?    Yes    Sometimes    No

2. Have you been able to go into more depth in these topics and projects?    Yes    Sometimes    No

3. Has the Workshop Program helped you learn study skills?    Yes    Sometimes    No

4. Has the Workshop Program helped you learn higher level thinking skills?    Yes    Sometimes    No

5. Has the Workshop Program helped you become more responsible at school?    Yes    Sometimes    No

6. Are you challenged by the Workshop Program?    Yes    Sometimes    No

7. Are there opportunities for you to express your feelings and opinions?    Yes    Sometimes    No

8. Has the Workshop Program helped you develop respect for yourself?    Yes    Sometimes    No

9. Are there opportunities to express your creativity?    Yes    Sometimes    No

10. What do you like about the Workshop Program?  _____  _____

11. What would you change about the Workshop Program?  _____  _____

**Form 13.8** Parent Evaluation of University Workshops for Gifted Youth

We are collecting data to determine whether these programs have been effective in helping students reach their potential. Please answer the following questions and write your comments or suggestions on this survey to help us better evaluate our programs.

The information gathered from this survey will be analyzed by an outside evaluator and reported to teachers, parents, administrators, and school board members. You may or may not include your name, and all information will remain confidential. Throughout the survey, the University Workshops for Gifted Youth will be referred to as the "Workshop Program."

1 = *never or not good*
2 = *seldom or only partially true*
3 = *usually or generally true*
4 = *always or good*

Please rate the Workshop Program using the scale above.

| | 1 | 2 | 3 | 4 |
|---|---|---|---|---|
| 1. Degree to which the Workshop Program has made your child more interested in learning | 1 | 2 | 3 | 4 |
| 2. Degree to which the Workshop Program has helped your child become a better evaluator of his or her own work | 1 | 2 | 3 | 4 |
| 3. Suitability of the identification method by which your child was selected for the Workshop Program | 1 | 2 | 3 | 4 |
| 4. Opportunity for your student to select topics for study that are of interest to him or her | 1 | 2 | 3 | 4 |
| 5. Opportunity for your child to pursue topics more in depth | 1 | 2 | 3 | 4 |
| 6. Extent to which the Workshop Program has helped your student use higher order thinking skills | 1 | 2 | 3 | 4 |
| 7. Extent to which the Workshop Program has helped your student develop more individual responsibility | 1 | 2 | 3 | 4 |

| | | | | |
|---|---|---|---|---|
| 8. Degree to which your student has been challenged by the Workshop Program | 1 | 2 | 3 | 4 |
| 9. Your overall rating of the Workshop Program in terms of fulfilling your student's immediate educational needs | 1 | 2 | 3 | 4 |
| 10. Extent of the opportunities for your child to express his or her ideas | 1 | 2 | 3 | 4 |
| 11. Extent of opportunities for your child to express his or her feelings | 1 | 2 | 3 | 4 |
| 12. Extent to which the Workshop Program has helped your student develop his or her respect for self | 1 | 2 | 3 | 4 |
| 13. Extent to which the Workshop Program has helped your student develop respect for others | 1 | 2 | 3 | 4 |
| 14. Opportunities for your students to express creativity | 1 | 2 | 3 | 4 |
| 15. Extent to which the teachers for the Workshop Program are enthusiastic about their teaching in the program | 1 | 2 | 3 | 4 |
| 16. Extent to which the teachers for the Workshop Program demonstrate adequate knowledge of the content areas and techniques for instructing high-ability students | 1 | 2 | 3 | 4 |
| 17. Extent to which your child has been able to participate in extracurricular activities as well as be successful in school | 1 | 2 | 3 | 4 |
| 18. Extent to which you see the teacher adjusting the curriculum and instructional strategies for your child's level of ability or strengths | 1 | 2 | 3 | 4 |

19. What are some of the positive aspects of the Workshop Program?  _____

20. If you could change the Workshop Program, what would you do?  _____

Forms 13.6 through 13.8 were developed for the evaluation of a summer workshop program. Input was gathered from teachers, parents, and students to ascertain areas needing improvement.

Assessment of gifted programs by the stakeholders and assessment of students, teachers, and counselors in the program serve to inform decisions at all levels. Teachers can adjust their curriculum design and activities based on the input from students in their courses. Program developers can modify various aspects of the overall program based on input from multiple sources. Thoughtful assessment practices will have positive effects on out-of-school programming for gifted students.

## NOTE

1.  Headings adapted from Ellwein (1992).

# Concluding Thoughts

## Looking Ahead

*Joan Franklin Smutny*

The authors in this book have examined gifted programs *within* school systems (i.e., those operated by school administration and funded by the district) and those *outside*—often funded by universities or institutes. Because readers may be coming at this subject as teachers or administrators in a school or as an independent group outside any district, we wanted to include both in this book. Program directors in both situations have similar challenges and responsibilities in designing and implementing curricula, communicating with parents, and assessing the effectiveness of their services to the gifted and their families.

Yet there are differences worth noting. For example, gifted coordinators of in-school programs may not have to concern themselves about budgets or finding space for classes to the extent that independent ones do. Supplemental weekend or summer program administrators have to spend a lot of time on logistics, budgets, and funding. On the other hand, in-school programs sometimes lack the freedoms of supplemental programs, particularly in the kinds of classes they can offer and the time they spend with a group of students. Supplemental programs can also innovate and attempt to implement novel ideas without having to convince an entire administration or district.

Given the lack of support services for gifted children, both kinds of programs have a vital role to play for the nation's gifted students. But in order for these programs to ensure a better future for gifted education, they need to consider ways that they can share ideas and pool resources. Certainly, collaborations among the different programs would translate into greater opportunities for gifted children both inside and outside school. Giftedness is a full-time condition requiring more than a few stimulating classes. Programs that share information, expertise, and resources can accomplish much more for gifted students, their families, and the community.

Here are some examples. A program sponsored by a university could help a school launch a pull-out program. Conversely, a public school gifted program could help a new, university summer gifted program develop appropriate curriculum for high-ability students. Master teachers from a university program could team with teachers in a district to develop strategies for meeting the learning needs of gifted students in the regular classroom. Administrators from different programs, parents, and interested teachers could network to campaign for more funding from the state for gifted education in the schools.

Through networking, gifted programs within and outside the school district could also schedule a series of small lectures or seminars for parents, teachers, and administrators that would pull together the talents and expertise of the whole school community. This exchange of information and expertise would dispel some of the myths about gifted children and gifted education and would generate more support for both the school's program and supplemental programs sponsored by universities or institutes.

The two kinds of programs could enhance each other—one operating within the structure and curriculum demands of the school district and the other providing a wider range of courses, class activities, and learning formats. Over time, this kind of networking creates a larger safety net for students who might otherwise slip through the cracks. Collaborations between programs would be especially effective in meeting the needs of underserved gifted populations whose schools have less access to resources and information about gifted children.

In addition to such networking, programs also need to be places where both teachers and parents explore effective strategies for child advocacy. They need to address the question, How can we extend the benefits that children gain from our programs to their lives beyond this time-frame? For many parents, a gifted program may be the first time they have seen their children in an environment where teachers nurture their talents and encourage them to take risks, where they feel at home with peers and confident about themselves and their place in the world. Watching a child retreat back into a shell after a program ends often increases parents' apprehensions for the future and may make them question the long-term effectiveness of gifted programs.

Whether we happen to be a mentor, a parent, a friend, or a teacher, we need to be aware that gifted children are at risk of becoming underachievers and that their abilities—dazzling as they may appear—do not automatically ensure success and accomplishment. Though many of them are highly articulate and mature, gifted children lack the years of life experience that enable them to have a balanced perspective on their struggles in school and society. Many develop destructive thought patterns as a result of a perfectionism they cannot control, a heightened sensitivity to the opinions of others, and a heavy sense of self-doubt and self-criticism about everything they do.

Young people cannot negotiate these pitfalls on their own. They need the support and mentoring of an informed adult who can teach the life skills that are so vital to their development and success. Programs offer a rare opportunity for teachers, parents, administrators, and gifted education specialists to focus on current research and methods for effective child advocacy. Through workshops, seminars, and private counseling, programs could do far more to address specific problems facing gifted students from all cultural and socioeconomic backgrounds. Sharing their knowledge, insights, and experiences, parents and teachers can design coping strategies for students who are at greatest risk of underachieving. These efforts bear fruit. Each intervention on their behalf (however small) gives them courage to be themselves—to accept what they are and step boldly into a future that holds more promise for their talents and abilities.

*I want to reach*

*Dancer, Dancer*

*Out through your prism of glass*

*out and touch your ivory skin, your fan of magic you weave*

*in your steps you weave flowing from you*

*Dancer Dancer*

*As the music's silken rhythm glides under your slippers,*

*lifting you up to touch the clouds*

*Dancer*

*Dancer*

*Light as spreading ripples in clear waters*

*Graceful as the swirling fuchsia markings on*

*a majestic pair of fairy wings*

*Dancer*

*Dancer*

*Don't stay horridly that way*

*move, move, make me part of you*

—Kendall, Grade 5

# Other Resources

## References

Alencar, E. M. L. S. (1986). *Psicologia e educacao do superdotado* [Psychology and evaluation of the gifted]. São Paulo: EPU.

Alvino, J. (1985). *Parents' guide to raising a gifted child: Recognizing and developing your child's potential.* New York: Ballantine.

American Association for Gifted Children. (1978). *On being gifted.* New York: Walker and Company.

Assouline, S., & Lupkowski-Shoplik, A. (1997). Talent searches: A model for the discovery and development of academic talent. In N. Colangelo & G. A. Davis (Eds.), *Handbook of gifted education* (pp. 170-179). Boston: Allyn & Bacon.

Baldwin, A.Y. (2002). Lost and found: Achievers in urban schools. In J. F. Smutny (Ed.), *Underserved gifted populations.* Cresskill, NJ: Hampton.

Barbella, P., Kepner, J., & Schaeffer, R. L. (1995). *Exploring measurements.* Palo Alto, CA: Dale Seymour.

Baska, J. V. (1985). Appropriate curriculum for the gifted. In J. Feldhusen (Ed.), *Toward excellence in gifted education* (pp. 45-67). Denver, CO: Love.

Belgrad, S. F. (1998). Creating the most enabling environment for young gifted children. In J. F. Smutny (Ed.), *The young gifted child: Potential and promise, an anthology* (pp. 369-389). Cresskill, NJ: Hampton.

Borland, J. H., & Wright, L. (1994). Identifying young, potentially gifted, economically disadvantaged students. *Gifted Child Quarterly, 38*(4), 164-171.

Brady, P. (1997). *Gifted education: Personal observations and experiences.* Los Angeles: The Mirman School.

Burrill, G. (Ed.). (1994). *From home runs to housing costs: Data resources for teaching statistics.* Palo Alto, CA: Dale Seymour.

California Association for the Gifted (CAG). (1998a). *Advocacy in action: An advocacy handbook for gifted and talented education.* Whittier, CA: Author.

California Association for the Gifted (CAG). (1998b). *Joining forces: A guide to forming support organizations for gifted and talented children.* Whittier, CA: Author.

California Association for the Gifted (CAG). (Ed.). (1999). Issue highlight: Young gifted children [Special issue]. *Communicator, 30*(4).

Callahan, C. M. (2001). Evaluating learner and program outcomes in gifted education. In F. A. Karnes & S. M. Bean (Eds.), *Methods and materials for teaching the gifted* (pp. 253-298). Waco, TX: Prufrock.

Callahan, C. M., & Caldwell, M. S. (1999). *A practitioner's guide to evaluating programs for the gifted.* Washington, DC: National Association for Gifted Children.

Caplan, G. (1964). *Principles of preventive psychiatry.* New York: Basic Books.

Clark, B. (1988). *Growing up gifted* (3rd ed.). Columbus, OH: Charles E. Merrill.

Clark, B. (1992). *Growing up gifted* (4th ed.). Columbus, OH: Merrill.

Clark, B. (1997). *Growing up gifted: Developing the potential of children at home and at school* (5th ed.). Upper Saddle River, NJ: Prentice Hall.

Clark, G., & Zimmerman, E. (2001). Identifying artistically talented students in four rural communities in the United States. *Gifted Child Quarterly, 45,* 104-114.

Cline, S. (2000). *Giftedness has many faces: Multiple talents and abilities in the classroom.* Delray Beach, FL: Winslow.

C-MITES (Carnegie Mellon Institute for Talented Elementary Students). (2001). *Summer program 2001.* Pittsburgh, PA: Author.

Cohen, L. M. (1998). Facilitating the interest themes of young gifted children. In J. F. Smutny (Ed.), *The young gifted child: Potential and promise, an anthology* (pp. 317-339). Cresskill, NJ: Hampton.

Cohen, L. M., & Jipson, J. A. (1998). Conceptual models: Their role in early education for the gifted and talented. In J. F. Smutny (Ed.), *The young gifted child: Potential and promise, an anthology* (pp. 390-419). Cresskill, NJ: Hampton.

Colangelo, N., & Davis, G. (Eds.). (1991). *Handbook of gifted education.* Boston: Allyn & Bacon.

Colangelo, N., & Davis, G. (1997). *Handbook of gifted education.* Needham Heights, MA: Allyn & Bacon.

Coleman, L. J., & Cross, T. L. (2001). *Being gifted in school: An introduction to development, guidance, and teaching.* Waco, TX: Prufrock.

Coleman, M. R. (1995). Problem-based learning: A new approach for teaching gifted students. *Gifted Child Today, 18*(3), 18-19.

Cox, J., Daniel, N., & Boston, B. (1985). *Educating able learners: Programs and promising practices.* Austin: University of Texas Press.

Csikszentmihalyi, M. (1990). *Flow: The psychology of optimal experience.* New York: HarperCollins.

Davis, G., & Rimm, S. (1989). *Education of the gifted and talented.* Englewood Cliffs, NJ: Prentice Hall.

Davis, G. A., & Rimm, S. B. (1997). *Education of the gifted and talented* (4th ed.). Needham Heights, MA: Allyn & Bacon.

Dettmer, P. (1985). Gifted programs' scope, structure and evaluation. *Roeper Review, 7*(3), 146-152.

Drake, S. (1998). *Creating integrated curriculum.* Thousand Oaks, CA: Corwin.

Ehrlich, P., & Holdren, J. P. (1971, May 1). The lost genius debate. *Saturday Review.*

Ehrlich, V. Z. (1989). *Gifted children: A guide for parents and teachers.* New York: Trillium.

Ellwein, M. C. (1992, April). *Watching teachers watching students.* Paper presented at the annual meeting of the American Educational Research Association, San Francisco.

Emerson, R. W. (1844). Gifts. In *Essays: Second series* (pp. 67-76). Boston: James Munroe Press.

Enersen, D. (1993). Summer residential programs: Academics and beyond. *Gifted Child Quarterly, 37,* 169-176.

Erickson, H. L. (1998). *Concept-based curriculum and instruction: Teaching beyond the facts.* Thousand Oaks, CA: Corwin.

Esquivelle, G., & Houtz, J. C. (Eds.). (2000). *Creativity and giftedness in culturally diverse students.* Cresskill, NJ: Hampton.

Feiring, C., Louis, B., Ukeje, I., Lewis, M., & Leong, P. (1997, Summer). Early identification of gifted minority students in Newark, New Jersey. *Gifted Child Quarterly, 41,* 76-82.

Feldhusen, J. (1973). Practicum activities for students and gifted children in a university course. *Gifted Child Quarterly, 17,* 124-129.

Feldhusen, J. (1985). A conception of the field of gifted education. In J. Feldhusen (Ed.), *Toward excellence in gifted education* (pp. 15-28). Denver, CO: Love.

Feldhusen, J. (1991). Saturday and summer programs. In N. Colangelo & G. B. Davis (Eds.), *Handbook of gifted education* (pp. 197-208). Boston: Allyn & Bacon.

Feldhusen, J., & Baska, L. (1985) Identification and assessment of the gifted and talented. In J. Feldhusen (Ed.), *Toward excellence in gifted education* (pp. 69-82). Denver, CO: Love.

Feldhusen, J., & Moon, S. M. (1992, Spring). Grouping gifted students: Issues and concerns. *Gifted Child Quarterly, 36*(2), 63-67.

Feldhusen, J., VanTassel-Baska, J., & Seeley, K. (Eds.). (1989). *Excellence in educating the gifted.* Denver, CO: Love.

Fisher, M. (1992). Early childhood education for the gifted: The need for intense study and observation. *Illinois Association for the Gifted Children Journal, 11,* 6-9.

Ford, D. Y. (1996). *Reversing underachievement among gifted Black students: Promising practices and programs.* New York: Teachers College Press.

Fowler, M. (1990). The diet cola test. *Science Scope, 13*(4), 32-34.

Freeman, C. (2001). *Nim, variations and strategies: Serious math with a simple name.* San Luis Obispo, CA: Dandy Lion.

Galbraith, J. (1983). *The gifted kid's survival guide.* Minneapolis, MN: Free Spirit.

Galbraith, J. (1999). *The gifted kids' survival guide: For ages 10 and under* (Rev. ed.). Minneapolis, MN: Free Spirit.

Gallagher, J., & Bristol, M. (1989). Families of young handicapped children. In M. Wang, M. Reynolds, & H. Walberg (Eds.), *The handbook of special education, research, and practices* (Vol. 3, pp. 180-191). Oxford, England: Pergamon.

Gallagher, J., & Gallagher, S. (1994). *Teaching the gifted child* (4th ed.). Boston: Allyn & Bacon.

Gallagher, S. A., & Stepien, W. J. (1996). Content acquisition in problem-based learning: Depth versus breadth in American studies. *Journal for the Education of the Gifted, 19,* 257-275.

Gardner, H. (1993). *Multiple intelligences: The theory in practice.* New York: Basic Books.

Gardner, H. (1999). *Intelligence reframed: Multiple intelligences for the 21st century.* New York: Basic Books.

Gnanadesikan, M., Schaeffer, R. L., & Swift, J. (1987). *The art and techniques of simulation.* Palo Alto, CA: Dale Seymour.

Goleman, D. (1995). *Emotional intelligence: Why it can matter more than IQ.* New York: Bantam.

Gordon, T. (1970). *P.E.T. Parent effectiveness training.* New York: Wyden.

Gross, M. U. M. (1993). *Exceptionally gifted children*. London: Routledge Kegan Paul.

Gross, M. U. M. (1999). Small poppies: Highly gifted children in the early years. *Roeper Review, 21*(3), 207-214.

Hackney, H. (1981). The gifted child, the family, and the school. *Gifted Child Quarterly, 25*(2), 51-54.

Hoxby, C. M. (2000, August). *Peer effects in the classroom: Learning from gender and race variation*. Working Paper 7868, National Bureau of Economic Research, Cambridge, MA.

Huff, D. (1954). *How to lie with statistics*. New York: Penguin.

Johnsen, S. (2000). Glyptodonts: A summer camp experience. *Gifted Child Today, 23*(3), 5.

Johnson, N. (1989). *The faces of gifted*. Marion, IL: Creative Learning Consultants.

Johnson, N. (1995). *Active questioning*. Beavercreek, OH: Pieces of Learning.

Kaplan, S. (1989). Competency cluster for the teachers of the gifted. *CAG Communicator, 19*(4), 13-14.

Karnes, F. A., & Bean, S. M. (1995). *Girls and young women inventing: Twenty true stories about inventors plus how you can be one yourself*. Minneapolis, MN: Free Spirit.

Karnes, M. B. (Ed.). (1983). *The underserved: Our gifted young children*. Reston, VA: Council for Exceptional Children.

Kerr, B. A. (1997). *Smart girls: A new psychology of girls, women, and giftedness*. Scottsdale, AZ: Gifted Psychology Press.

Kingore, B. (1993). *Portfolios: Enriching and assessing all students, identifying the gifted, Grades K-6*. Des Moines, IA: Leadership Publishers.

Kingore, B. (1995). Portfolios for young children. *Understanding Our Gifted, 7*(3), 10-12.

Kitano, M. (1982, May). Young gifted children: Strategies for preschool teachers. *Young Children*, pp. 14-24.

Kitano, M. (1986, July-August). Counseling gifted preschoolers. *Gifted Child Today*, pp. 20-25.

Knopper, D. (1995). *Parent education: Parents as partners*. Boulder, CO: Open Space Communications.

Kohl, H. (1967). *36 children*. New York: New American Library.

Kozol, P. (1991). *Savage inequalities*. New York: The Trumpet Club.

Kulik, J., & Kulik, C.-L. (1991). Ability grouping and gifted students. In N. Colangelo & G. A. Davis (Eds.), *Handbook of gifted education* (pp. 215-228). Boston: Allyn & Bacon.

L'Abate, L., & Weinstein, S. E. (1987). *Structure enrichment programs for couples and families*. New York: Brunner & Mazel.

Landrum, M. S., Callahan, C. A., & Shaklee, B. D. (Eds.). (2001). *Aiming for excellence: Annotations to the NAGC Pre-K–Grade 12 gifted program standards*. Washington, DC: National Association for Gifted Children.

Landwehr, J. M., Swift, J., & Watkins, A. E. (1987). *Exploring surveys and information from samples*. Palo Alto, CA: Dale Seymour.

Landwehr, J. M., & Watkins, A. E. (1996). *Exploring data*. Palo Alto, CA: Dale Seymour.

Lazear, D. (1994). *Multiple intelligence approaches to assessment: Solving the assessment conundrum*. Tucson, AZ: Zephyr.

Leimbach, J. (1991). *Primarily thinking*. San Luis Obispo, CA: Dandy Lion Publications.

Leimbach, J., & Eckert, S. (1996). *Primary book reporter: Independent reading for young learners*. San Luis Obispo, CA: Dandy Lion.

LeVine, E. S., & Kitano, M. K. (1998). Helping young gifted children reclaim their strengths. In J. F. Smutny (Ed.), *The young gifted child: Potential and promise, an anthology* (pp. 282-294). Cresskill, NY: Hampton.

Louis, B., & Lewis, M. (1992). Parental beliefs about giftedness in young children and their relation to actual ability level. *Gifted Child Quarterly, 36*(1), 27-31.

Lupkowski, A., & Assouline, S. (1992). *Jane and Johnny love math: Recognizing and encouraging mathematical talent in elementary students*. Unionville, NY: Trillium.

Mahoney, A. S. (1998). In search of the gifted identity: From abstract concept to workable counseling constructs. *Roeper Review, 20*(3), 222-226.

Maker, C. J. (1982). *Curriculum development for the gifted*. Austin, TX: PRO-ED.

Marland, S. (1972). *Education of the gifted and talented*. Report to the Congress of the United States by the U.S. Commissioner of Education. Washington, DC: Government Printing Office.

Martinson, R. (1962). Special programs for gifted pupils. *Bulletin of the California State Department of Education, 31*(1), 1-3.

Meador, K. (1997). *Creative thinking and problem solving for young learners*. Englewood, CO: Teacher Ideas Press/Libraries Unlimited.

Meador, K. S. (1998). *Creative thinking and problem solving for young learners*. Englewood, CO: Libraries Unlimited.

Monks, F. J., & Ypenburg, J. (1993). *Unser Kind ist hochbegabt: Ein Leitfaden für Eltern und Lehrer* [Our child is gifted: A guide for parents and teachers]. Munich: Reinhardt.

Moon, T. R., Callahan, C. M., & Tomlinson, C. A. (1999). The effects of mentoring relationships on preservice teachers' attitudes toward academically diverse students. *Gifted Child Quarterly, 43,* 56-62.

Moore, N. D., & Moore, S. D. (1997, July). *Gifted students' perceptions of meaningful academic work*. Paper presented at the Association for Psychological Type Biennial International Conference, Boston.

Moro, M. L. F. (1987). *Aprendizagem operatoria: A interacao social da crianca* [Operative learning: The social interaction of the child]. São Paulo: Cortez: Autores Associados; Curitiba: Sciencia et Labor.

National Association for Gifted Children (NAGC). (1994). *Competencies needed by teachers of gifted and talented students*. Washington, DC: Author.

National Research Council. (1999). *How people learn: Brain, mind, experience, and school*. Washington, DC: National Academy Press.

National Society for the Study of Education. (1979). *The gifted and the talented*. Chicago: University of Chicago Press.

Newman, C. M., Obremski, T. E., & Schaeffer, R. L. (1987). *Exploring probability*. Palo Alto, CA: Dale Seymour.

Nitko, A. J. (1996). *Educational assessment of students*. Englewood Cliffs, NJ: Prentice Hall.

Olenchak, F. R. (1998). *They say my kid's gifted: Now what?* Waco, TX: Prufrock.

Ordem Rosacruz—AMORC. (1989). *Educacao rosacruz integrada* [Rosocruz integrated education]. Curitiba: Grande Loja do Brasil, AMORC.

Oszewski-Kubilius, P. (1997). Special summer and Saturday programs for gifted students. In N. Colangelo & G. A. Davis (Eds.), *Handbook of gifted education* (pp. 180-188). Boston: Allyn & Bacon.

Oszewski-Kubilius, P., Grant, B., & Seibert, C. (1993). Social support systems and the disadvantaged gifted: A framework for developing programs and services. *Roeper Review, 17*, 20-25.

Otto, H. A. (Ed.). (1976). *Marriage and family enrichment.* Nashville, TN: Abingdon.

Parke, B. (Ed.). (1989). *Program standards of the gifted and talented.* Reston, VA: Association for the Gifted.

Parker, J. P. (1989). *Instructional strategies for teaching the gifted.* Boston: Allyn & Bacon.

Passow, H. (1982). *Differentiated curricula for the gifted/talented.* Paper prepared to reflect the majority opinion of the Curriculum Council and sponsored by the N/S-LTI-G/T, Ventura County Superintendent of Schools Office, Ventura, CA.

Passow, H. A. (1992). *Growing up gifted and talented: Schools, families and communities.* Hong Kong: Proceedings of the Second Asian Conference on Giftedness.

Paulos, J. A. (1990). *Innumeracy: Mathematical illiteracy and its consequences.* New York: Vintage.

Paulos, J. A. (1996). *A mathematician reads the newspaper.* New York: Anchor.

Perret-Clermont, A. (1978). *A construcao da inteligencia pela interacao social* [The construction of intelligence through social interaction]. Trans. by E. Godinh. Lisbon: Socincultur.

Piirto, J. (1998a). *Talented children and adults: Their development and education* (2nd ed.). Upper Saddle River, NJ: Prentice Hall.

Piirto, J. (1998b). *Understanding those who create.* Scottsdale, AZ: Gifted Psychology Press.

Piirto, J. (1999). *Talented children and adults: Their development and education* (2nd ed.). Upper Saddle River, NJ: Prentice Hall.

Piskurich, P. J., & Lupkowski-Shoplik, A. (1998). Carnegie Mellon weekend workshops: Weekend fun. *Gifted Child Today, 21*(4), 14-19.

Porter, L. (1999). *Gifted young children: A guide for teachers and parents.* St. Leonards NSW, Australia: Allen & Unwin.

Rea, D. W. (2000). Optimal motivation for talent development. *Journal for the Education of the Gifted, 23*, 187-216.

Reis, S., Burns, D. E., & Renzulli, J. (1992). *Curriculum compacting: The complete guide to modifying the regular curriculum for high ability students.* Mansfield Center, CT: Creative Learning Press.

Renzulli, J. (1977). *The enrichment triad model: A guide for developing defensible programs for the gifted.* Mansfield Center, CT: Creative Learning Press.

Renzulli, J. S., & Reis, S. M. (1985). *The schoolwide enrichment model: A comprehensive plan for educational excellence.* Mansfield Center, CT: Creative Learning Press.

Renzulli, J. S., & Reis, S. M. (1986). The enrichment triad/revolving door model: A schoolwide plan for the development of creative productivity. In J. S. Renzulli (Ed.), *Systems and models for developing programs for the gifted and talented* (pp. 216-266). Mansfield, CT: Creative Learning Press.

Renzulli, J. S., & Reis, S. M. (1991). Building advocacy through program design, student productivity and public relations. *Gifted Child Quarterly, 35*(4), 182-187.

Renzulli, J. S., & Reis, S. M. (1997). The schoolwide enrichment model: New directions for developing high-end learning. In N. Colangelo & G. A. Davis (Eds.), *Handbook for gifted education* (pp. 136-154). Needham Heights, MA: Allyn & Bacon.

Renzulli, J. S., Reid, B. D., & Gubbins, E. J. (1992). *Setting an agenda: Research priorities for the gifted and talented through year 2000*. Storrs: University of Connecticut, National Research Center on the Gifted and Talented.

Renzulli, J. S., & Smith, L. H. (1978). *The learning styles inventory*. Mansfield Center, CT: Creative Learning Press.

Rimm, S. (1983). *How to parent so children will learn*. Watertown, WI: Apple Publishing.

Rimm, S. (1986). *Underachievement syndrome: Causes and cures*. Watertown, WI: Apple Publishing.

Rimm, S. (1991). Underachievement and superachievement: Flip sides of the same psychological coin. In N. Colangelo & G. A. Davis (Eds.), *Handbook of gifted education* (pp. 328-343). Boston: Allyn & Bacon.

Rimm, S. (1995). *Keys to parenting the gifted child*. New York: Barron's Educational Series.

Rivero, L. (2000). *Gifted education comes home: A case for self-directed homeschooling*. Manassas, VA: Gifted Education Press.

Robinson, A., & Kolloff, P. B. (1994). Developing secondary thematic units. In J. B. Hansen & S. M. Hoover (Eds.), *Talent development: Theories and practice* (pp. 153-183). Dubuque, IA: Kendall/Hunt.

Rupp, R. (1998). *The complete home learning source book*. New York: Three Rivers.

Sabatella, M. L. P. (1995). *Instituto para otimizacao da aprendizagem: Uma alternativa educacional para alunos superdotcdos e talentosos* [Institute of learning optimization: An educational alternative for gifted and talented children]. Unpublished master's thesis, Federal University of Parana, Curitiba, Brazil

Samara, J., & Curry, J. (Eds.). (1994). *Developing units for primary students*. Bowling Green, KY: KAGE.

Saunders, J. (1991). *Bringing out the best: A resource guide for parents of young gifted children*. Minneapolis, MN: Free Spirit.

Schwartz, W. (1997). *How to recognize and develop your children's special talents* (Eric Digest 122). New York: ERIC Clearinghouse on Urban Education. (ERIC Document Reproduction Service No. EDO-UD-97-3)

Seagoe, M. (1959, October 28). A talk to parents.

Seeley, K. R. (1979). Competencies for teachers of gifted and talented children. *Journal of the Education of the Gifted, 3*(1), 7-13.

Seeley, K. R. (1985). Facilitators for gifted learners. In J. Feldhusen (Ed.), *Toward excellence in gifted education* (pp. 105-129). Denver, CO: Love.

Sellen, D. F., & Birch, J. W. (1980). *Educating gifted and talented learners*. Ruckville, MD: Aspen Systems Corporation.

Shaklee, B. (1995). Creating positive learning environments: Young gifted children at home and in school. *Understanding Our Gifted, 7*(3), 8-9.

Sisk, D. (1987). *Creative teaching of the gifted*. New York: McGraw-Hill.

Sisk, D. A., & Torrance, E. P. (Eds.). (2000). *On the edge and keeping on the edge*. Westport, CT: Ablex.

Smutny, J. (1998a). *Gifted girls*. Bloomington, IN: Phi Delta Kappa Educational Foundation.

Smutny, J. (Ed.). (1998b). *The young gifted child: Potential and promise, an anthology*. Cresskill, NJ: Hampton.

Smutny, J. (2001). *Stand up for your gifted child*. Minneapolis, MN: Free Spirit.

Smutny, J. (Ed.). (2002). *Underserved gifted populations*. Cresskill, NJ: Hampton.

Smutny, J., & Blocksom, R. (1990). *Education of the gifted: Programs and perspectives.* Bloomington, IN: Phi Delta Kappa Educational Foundation.

Smutny, J., Veenker, K., & Veenker, S. (1989). *Your gifted child: How to recognize and develop the special talents in your child from birth to age seven.* New York: Ballantine.

Smutny, J., Walker, S., & Meckstroth, E. (1997). *Teaching young gifted children in the regular classroom: Identifying, nurturing, and challenging ages 4-9.* Minneapolis, MN: Free Spirit.

Staehle, D. (2000). Taking a different path: A mother's reflections on homeschooling. *Roeper Review, 22,* 270-271.

Stephens, K. R., & Karnes, F. A. (2000). Classroom to community: Student products as the link. *Gifted Child Today, 23*(6), 14-19.

Taylor, R. (1991). *Reshaping the curriculum: Integrate, differentiate, compact, and think.* Oakbrook, IL: Curriculum Design for Excellence.

Thompson, M. C. (1996). OGC research review: Rigor. *Our Gifted Children, 21,* 5-7.

Thompson, M. C., & Thompson, M. B. (1996). The rigor of foreign language study. *Our Gifted Children, 21,* 9-18.

Tomlinson, C. A. (1995). *Differentiating instruction for advanced learners in the mixed-ability middle school classroom* (ERIC Digest E536). Reston, VA: ERIC Clearinghouse on Disabilities and Gifted Education. (ERIC Document Reproduction Service No. ED 389 141)

Tomlinson, C. A. (1998). *How to differentiate instruction in mixed-ability classrooms* (2nd ed.). Alexandria, VA: Association for Supervision and Curriculum Development.

Tomlinson, C. A., Coleman, M. R., Allan, S., Udall, A., & Landrum, M. (1996). Interface between gifted education and general education: Toward communication, cooperation, and collaboration. *Gifted Child Quarterly, 40*(3), 165-171.

Tomlinson, C. A., Kaplan, S. N., Renzulli, J. S., Purcell, J., Leppien, J., & Burns, D. (2002). *The parallel curriculum: A design to develop high potential and challenge high-ability learners.* Thousand Oaks, CA: Corwin.

Torrance, E. P. (1962). *Guiding creative talent.* Englewood Cliffs, NJ: Prentice Hall.

Torrance, E. P. (1977). *Discovery and nurturance of giftedness in the culturally different.* Reston, VA: Council for Exceptional Children.

Torrance, E. P. (1998). Talent among children who are economically disadvantaged or culturally different. In J. F. Smutny (Ed.), *The young gifted child: Potential and promise, an anthology* (pp. 95-118). Cresskill, NJ: Hampton.

Torrance, E. P., Goff, K., & Satterfield, N. B. (1997). *Multicultural mentoring of the gifted and talented.* Waco, TX: Prufrock.

Torrance, E. P., Murdock, M., & Fletcher, D. (1996). *Creative problem solving through role playing.* Pretoria, South Africa: Benedic.

Torrance, E. P., & Safter, H. T. (1990). *Incubation model of teaching: Getting beyond aha!* Buffalo, NY: Bearly Limited.

Treffinger, D. J. (1980). *Encouraging creative learning for the gifted and talented: A handbook of methods and techniques.* Los Angeles: National/State Leadership Training Institute on the Gifted and Talented.

Van Tassel-Baska, J. (1992). *Planning effective curriculum for gifted learners.* Denver, CO: Love.

Van Tassel-Baska, J. (1993). *Comprehensive curriculum for gifted learners.* Boston: Allyn & Bacon.

Van Tassel-Baska, J. (1996). The process of talent development. In J. VanTassel-Baska, D. T. Johnson, & L. N. Boyce (Eds.), *Developing verbal talent* (pp. 3-22). Boston: Allyn & Bacon.

Van Tassel-Baska, J. (1997). What matters in curriculum for gifted learners: Reflections on theory, research, and practice. In N. Colangelo & G. A. Davis (Eds.), *Handbook for gifted education* (pp. 126-135). Needham Heights, MA: Allyn & Bacon.

Van Tassel-Baska, J. (1998a). Appropriate curriculum for the talented learner. In J. VanTassel-Baska (Ed.), *Excellence in educating gifted and talented learners* (pp. 339-362). Denver, CO: Love.

Van Tassel-Baska, J. (1998b). Characteristics and needs of talented learners. In J. VanTassel-Baska (Ed.), *Excellence in educating gifted and talented learners* (pp. 173-192). Denver, CO: Love.

Van Tassel-Baska, J., Johnson, D. T., & Boyce, L. N. (Eds.). (1996). *Developing verbal talent: Ideas and strategies for teachers of elementary and middle school students.* Boston: Allyn & Bacon.

Vydra, J., & Leimbach, J. (1998). Planning curriculum for young gifted children. In J. F. Smutny (Ed.), *The young gifted child: Potential and promise, an anthology* (pp. 462-475). Cresskill, NJ: Hampton.

Warner, J., & Gardner, H. (1986). The crystallizing experience: Discovering an intellectual gift. In R. J. Sternberg & J. E. Davidson (Eds.), *Conceptions of giftedness* (pp. 306-330). New York: Cambridge University Press.

Webb, J. T. (1995). Cultivating courage, creativity and caring. In M. W. Katzko & F. J. Monks (Eds.), *Nurturing talent: Individual needs and social ability* (pp. 129-138). Assen, Netherlands: Van Gorcum.

Webb, J., & DeVries, A. (1993). *Training manual for facilitators of Seng Model guided discussion groups.* Dayton: Ohio Psychology Press.

Webb, J. T., Meckstroth, E. A., & Tolan, S. S. (1982). *Guiding the gifted child.* Dayton: Ohio Psychology Press.

Wiggins, G., & McTighe, J. (1998). *Understanding by design.* Alexandria, VA: Association for Supervision and Curriculum Development.

Winebrenner, S. (2001). *Teaching gifted kids in the regular classroom* (Rev. ed.). Minneapolis, MN: Free Spirit.

Wormser, R. (1991). *Lifers: Learn the truth at the expense of our sorrow.* New York: Julian 1313.

## *Organizations*

California Association for the Gifted
15141 E. Whittier Blvd., Suite 510
Whittier, CA 90603
562-789-9933
www.cagifted.org

The Center for Gifted
National-Louis University
2840 Sheridan Road
Evanston, IL 60201

847-256-5150, ext. 2150
www.centerforgifted.com

Center for Talented Youth
Johns Hopkins University
3400 North Charles Street
Baltimore, MD 21218
410-516-0337
www.jhu.edu/~gifted/

Council for Exceptional Children (CEC)
1110 North Glebe Road, Suite 300
Arlington, VA 22201-5704
1-888-232-7733
www.cec.sped.org

Educational Assessment Service, Inc.
W6050 Apple Road
Watertown, WI 53098
1-800-795-7466
www.sylviarimm.com

ERIC Clearinghouse on Disabilities and Gifted Education
1110 North Glebe Road
Arlington, VA 22201-5704
1-800-328-0272
www.ericec.org

Gifted Development Center
1452 Marion Street
Denver, CO 80218
303-837-8378
www.gifteddevelopment.com

Hollingworth Center for Highly Gifted Children
827 Center Avenue, #282
Dover, NH 03820-2506
www.hollingworth.org

Illinois Association for Gifted Children (IAGC)
800 East Northwest Highway
Suite 610
Palatine, IL 60067-6512
847-963-1892
www.iagcgifted.org

National Association for Gifted Children (NAGC)
1707 L Street NW, Suite 550
Washington, D.C. 20036
202-785-4268
www.nagc.org

The National Foundation for Gifted and Creative Children
395 Diamond Hill Road
Warwick, RI 02886
401-738-0937
www.nfgcc.org

National Research Center on the Gifted and Talented (NRC/GT)
University of Connecticut
2131 Hillside Road, Unit 3007
Storrs, CT 06269
860-486-4676
www.gifted.uconn.edu/nrcgt.html

National Women's History Project
3343 Industrial Drive, Suite 4
Santa Rosa, CA 95403
707-636-2888
www.nwhp.org

Texas Association for the Gifted and Talented
406 East Eleventh Street
Suite 310
Austin, TX 78701-2617
512-499-8248
www.txgifted.org

Torrance Center for Creative Studies
Department of Educational Psychology
323 Alderhold Hall
University of Georgia
Athens, GA 30602-7146
706-542-5104
www.coe.uga.edu/torrance

## *Publishers and Publications*

Corwin Press
    A Sage Publications Company
    2455 Teller Road

Thousand Oaks, CA 91320
805-499-9774
www.corwinpress.com

Corwin Press publishes research-based, strategy-driven resources for K-12 educators, and is an excellent resource for high-quality professional books and videos. In addition to this book, Corwin also publishes *The Parallel Curriculum: A Design to Develop High Potential and Challenge High-Ability Learners* (Tomlinson, Kaplan, Renzulli, Purcell, Leppien, and Burns) as a service publication for the National Association for Gifted Children.

Creative Learning Press
P.O. Box 320
Mansfeld Center, CT 06250
1-888-518-8004
www.creativelearningpress.com

Creative Learning Press provides a variety of manuals and activity books for teachers working with gifted children, including Renzulli and Reis's best-selling *Schoolwide Enrichment Model* and Reis's *Work Left Undone: Choices and Compromises of Talented Females*. It offers an extraordinary Mentors-in-Print section with a wide range of stimulating, hands-on, how-to books for gifted children at all grade levels.

Critical Thinking Books and Software
P.O. Box 448
Pacific Grove, CA 93950
1-800-458-4849
www.criticalthinking.com

This press produces the largest selection of high-quality critical thinking products for kindergarten through adult education. Its products aim to improve performance, encourage students at all ability levels, and extend achievement and success.

Dandy Lion Publications
3563 Sueldo, Suite L
San Luis Obispo, CA 93401
1-800-776-8032
www.dandylionbooks.com

Dandy Lion is a leading publisher of educational teaching materials that stresses development of creative and critical thinking for students in Grades K through 8. It presents innovative methods for teaching all subjects and is ideal for teachers in gifted and talented programs, teachers in regular classrooms, homeschoolers, and parents.

*Educational Opportunity Guide: A Directory of Programs for the Gifted*
Duke University Talent Identification Program
P.O. Box 90747
Durham, NC 27708
919-684-3847
www.tip.duke.edu

Free Spirit Publishing
217 Fifth Avenue North, Suite 200
Minneapolis, MN 55401-1299
1-800-735-7323
www.freespirit.com

Free Spirit is an award-winning publisher of nonfiction resources for children and teens, parents, educators, and counselors. It develops a variety of research-based and user-friendly materials on topics such as self-esteem and self-awareness, stress management, school success, creativity, friends and family, peacemaking, social action, and special needs (i.e., gifted and talented, learning differences).

*Gifted Education Communicator* (formerly known as *Communicator*), featuring articles by national leaders in the field, parent-to-parent articles, and hands-on curriculum. Published by the California Association for the Gifted (see entry under "Organizations").

Gifted Education Press
10201 Yuma Court
P.O. Box 1586
Manassas, VA 20108
703-369-5017
www.giftedpress.com

This press publishes books and periodicals on educating gifted children. It offers an extraordinary range of innovative materials for teachers, parents, homeschoolers, and students on all subjects at all grade levels. Press distributes materials in school districts across the nation.

Great Potential Press, Inc.
P.O. Box 5057
Scottsdale, AZ 85261
602-954-4200
www.giftedpsychologypress.com

Great Potential Press publishes books for parents, teachers, counselors, and educators of gifted and talented children. It focuses on subjects such as guiding gifted students, creativity, college planning, self-esteem, legal issues, girls, mentorship, parent advice, and more.

*Illinois Association for Gifted Children Journal* is a yearly publication that features articles on specific topics such as underserved populations, young gifted children, and teaching strategies for gifted students in the regular classroom. See entry on Illinois Association for the Gifted Children.

New Moon Publishing
P.O. Box 3620
Duluth, MN 55803
1-800-381-4743
www.newmoon.org

New Moon publishes *New Moon: The Magazine for Girls and Their Dreams*, *New Moon Network: For Adults Who Care About Girls*, books for girls, and curricula and learning activities for all grades that correspond with each issue of *New Moon*. This is an invaluable resource for teachers, homeschoolers, and girls' group leaders.

Open Space Communications
Box 18268
1900 Folsom, Suite 108
Boulder, CO 80308
1-800-494-6178
www.openspacecomm.com

A Colorado-based company that serves those who live and work with gifted children. Produces books and tapes and also publishes the outstanding journal for teachers and parents, *Understanding Our Gifted.*

*Parenting for High Potential* is a quarterly magazine for parents published by the National Association for Gifted Children. It includes suggestions for activities to do with your child as well as the latest Web sites, technology, and educational toys, all reviewed by experts in the field. See entry on NAGC.

Pieces of Learning
Division of Creative Learning Consultants
1990 Market Road
Marion, IL 62959
1-800-729-5137
www.piecesoflearning.com

Pieces of Learning is a publisher and producer of K through 12 supplementary enrichment activity books, resource books, and parenting and staff development videos. Topic areas include critical and creative thinking, questioning skills, and materials for subjects such as language arts, math, writing, literature, thematic learning, research, and much more.

Prufrock Press
  P.O. Box 8813
  Waco, TX 76714-8813
  1-800-998-2208
  www.prufrock.com

  Prufrock publishes innovative products and materials supporting the education of gifted and talented children. It offers teachers and parents of gifted children a comprehensive online education resource and a listing of gifted children links and products, gifted education magazines (e.g., *Gifted Child Today*), research journals, identification instruments, books, and more.

*Skipping Stones: A Multicultural Children's Magazine*
  P.O. Box 3939
  Eugene, OR 97403
  541-342-4956
  www.treelink.com/skipping/main.htm

  *Skipping Stones* is a nonprofit children's magazine that encourages cooperation, creativity, and celebration of cultural and environmental richness. An award-winning resource for multicultural and global education, it provides a forum for sharing ideas and experiences among children from different backgrounds.

*TEMPO* is a journal published four times a year by the Texas Association for the Gifted and Talented. The journal focuses on gifted education and features articles on a variety of themes such as leadership, identification, and homeschooling. See entry on Texas Association for the Gifted and Talented under "Organizations."

Thinking Caps
  P.O. Box 26239
  Phoenix, AZ 85068
  602-870-1527

  This publisher provides educational materials for the gifted designed specifically for classroom teachers. Most of the materials are based on Bloom's taxonomy.

Tin Man Press
  P.O. Box 11409
  Stanwood, WA 97440

1-800-676-0459

www.tinmanpress.com

This press publishes original thinking skills materials for the elementary grades that apply to a broad range of enrichment applications and in gifted programs. They are particularly appealing to inventive thinkers.

Zephyr Press

3316 North Chapel Avenue

Tucson, AZ 85716

520-322-5090

www.zephyrpress.com

Zephyr Press publishes educational materials focusing on the multiple intelligences theory. Activities within products integrate disciplines so that the learning is more meaningful. Designed for educators or parents, tools are practical, easy to use, and incorporate latest research.

# *Index*